TRIBULATION HAS BEGUN

By

Keisha G Knight

Copyright © 2022 Winniebell Publishing

All rights reserved.

All rights reserved. No part of this publication may be reproduced, stored or transmitted in any form or by any means, electronic, mechanical, photocopying, recording, scanning, or otherwise without written permission from the publisher. It is illegal to copy this book, post it to a website, or distribute it by any other means without permission.

Book Trailer

https://youtu.be/Mk6PHVbBaO4

TABLE OF CONTENTS

CHAPTER ONE 6

Covid; What is it 6

CHAPTER TWO 51

Follow up 2021 51

CHAPTER THREE 63

Tribulation.. 63

BIBLIOGRAPHY 77

BOOK FEEDBACK

I am thrilled, yet humbled and broken by the originality and precision of this book. The author demystifies the underworking of the evil camp and exposed their master plan. The author's ability to capture and pinpoint the occurrence of past events validates the likelihood of her future predictions. The author has been used mightily by God to convey the warning of the end time and to reveal, beforehand, the underworking of the devil. She accurately narrated the account of her revelation with God, by dating the events, and clearly explaining the trajectory of it all. The author is a prolific writer endowed with a strong creative expressive writing style. Each chapter carefully and concisely exposed me to the long-awaited plot of the devil and his future intentions against the children of God and mankind in general. The narrative technique of the author would leave you with introspection and enlightenment. Tribulation Has Begun exhibits balanced artistry of suspense and artistic candle and puts the author among the exalted league of those who bore the message of God. Readers will get a firsthand account of the author's opinion on Covid-19 and its role in the end-time prophecies. Further, readers will get to read about the author's conviction, hunger, and thirst for God. With a strong message revealing Jesus is coming soon, the devil manipulating the church and government, and the need for churches, to lessen and harken unto the voice of God. The author, the lead character in this book, has taken the lead in telling all who would open this book about the interest of God in His children and importance of God in our life.
By Book Editor Doris_foster

CHAPTER ONE

Covid; What is it

Matthew 5:10-12 KJV
10 Blessed are those who are persecuted for righteousness' sake,
For theirs is the kingdom of heaven.
11 Blessed are you when they revile and persecute you, and say all kinds of evil against you falsely for My sake.
12 Rejoice and be exceedingly glad, for great is your reward in heaven, for so they persecuted the prophets who were before you. (NKJV)

KGK

I did a 21-day prayer and fasting in January 2020. Before I commenced the fast, I had this burden in my heart that gave me this strong conviction that God wanted to show and teach me something great. This is the summary I came up with at the end of January; after the prayer and fasting.
This revelation was on the 24th of January 2020. The scientific mathematical numerological research of the power to the universe is the blueprint of God's DNA that He implanted in us; FATHER, SON, HOLY SPIRIT △

2/2020 – Around the final week of February. I woke up one morning knowing I was given two numbers No. 2 & No.2 (2, 2)
During this week, God instructed me to go food shopping, He instructed that I made sure all

pantries were filled, and I was to complete shopping within two weeks.

I maxed out my credit cards and purchased a storage bin from Home Depot. I was also instructed to tell everyone the same. I was told that in two weeks, there was going to be a mass panic in the supermarkets and stores. I did just that, I told everyone that they are to always be prepared for disasters. We are to emulate the five wise virgins at all times.

In two weeks, it all started with the panic setting in… I was also instructed by God to stay inside after 3/5/2020. I was told not to have anyone from outside, come inside the house…. (Something to do with mass transit)

During my time in the shelter, I was busy with worshipping and the prayer line ministry. I kept my eyes focused on God. I was in the house with 92-year-old aunt Mavis. She repeatedly said that this plague is a sin, a culmination of the sins of man.

Of course, increased text and WhatsApp messages displayed people s thoughts, conspiracies, fear, worry, and death, which all flooded the airwaves. Of course, I did listen to a few, but I never pinpointed anything. I knew that through sin, we as human beings with great brains, do a lot, maybe even too much? I am not questioning science, for the record, I am a professional registered nurse with almost 30 years of experience. I ONLY LOOK TO GOD.

On 4/14/2020 – S*******'s Dad passed due to covid……too many deaths… My spirit cried to God, for the fate that had befallen mankind. There was uneasiness in my being. God shut my mouth and tongue. I was heavy…. and my spirit kept feeling the nudge indicating that something is not right. I asked in my spirit "What is it, God?"

On 4/17/2020 - 3:52 pm- My spirit told me; that mankind's ever-evolving scientific quests to know more and be able to do more has lifted us to a new level... The human flesh may not survive the shift in radiation frequencies unless some sort of protection is available (Vaccine)...

On 4/17/2020 – 6:00 pm- My spirit whispered to me that something was not right... I couldn't pinpoint it, but it said something... Then my spirit said to me; (oops… something is wrong. This is not a virus. These are high electromagnetic rays. A resultant effect of RADIATION and THERE IS NO VACCINE...

On 4/17/2020 – 6:30 pm- God instructed me to research the virus. It was an eye-opener and everything added up.

On 4/18/2020, at about 12:30 am – I got the summary of the research. This is WHERE GOD SENT ME - WHAT IS THIS?[1]

What **frequency does 5G** use? **High**-band spectrum is sometimes called millimeter wavelength (mm Wave) in the cellular industry, and it enables about 28 GHz of **frequency**. This is considerably faster than 4G networks, which use about 700 MHz-2500 MHz **frequency** to transfer information.

What radio frequency is harmful to humans?

The most restrictive limits on whole-body exposure are in the frequency range of 30-300 **MHz** where the human body absorbs RF energy most efficiently when the whole body is exposed.

What frequency is dangerous?
The most restrictive limits on whole-body exposure are in the **frequency** range of 30-300 MHz where the human body absorbs RF energy most efficiently when the whole body is exposed.

---

[1] https://www.google.com/search?sxsrf=ALeKk00A7Dzgv29b4zCeH9q67D6yx0kBiA%3A158718 4790331&ei=IoSaXpLtE4KJytMPnZa72AY&q=

In general, the reported effects of radiofrequency (RF) radiation on tissue and organ systems have been attributed to thermal interactions, although the existence of non-thermal effects at low field intensities, regardless, it is still a subject of active investigation.

Effects of electromagnetic fields exposure on the antioxidant defense system[2]

Technological devices have become essential components of daily life. However, their deleterious effects on the body, particularly on the nervous system, are well known. Electromagnetic fields (EMF) have various chemical effects, including causing deterioration in large molecules in cells and an imbalance in ionic equilibrium. Despite being essential for life, oxygen molecules can lead to the generation of hazardous by-products, known as reactive oxygen species (ROS), during biological reactions. These reactive oxygen species can damage cellular components such as proteins, lipids, and DNA. Antioxidant defense systems exist in order to keep free radical formation under control and to prevent their harmful effects on the biological system. A free radical formation can take place in various ways, including ultraviolet light, drugs, lipid

---

[2] https://www.ncbi.nlm.nih.gov/pmc/articles/PMC6025786/

oxidation, immunological reactions, radiation, stress, smoking, alcohol, and biochemical redox reactions. Oxidative stress occurs if the antioxidant defense system is unable to prevent the harmful effects of free radicals. Several studies have reported that exposure to EMF results in oxidative stress in many tissues of the body. Exposure to EMF is known to increase free radical concentrations and traceability and can affect the radical couple recombination. The purpose of this review was to highlight the impact of oxidative stress on antioxidant systems.

The biological impacts of EMF can be classified as thermal and non-thermal. Thermal effects are associated with the heat created by EMFs in a certain area. This mechanism occurs via an alteration in temperature deriving from radiofrequency (RF) fields. Every interaction between RF fields and living tissues may cause an energy transfer resulting in a temperature rise. The skin and other superficial tissues usually absorb the non-thermal radiations emitted by mobile phones; this causes an insignificant increase in the temperature of the brain or other organs in the body [2]. Nonthermal mechanisms are those that are not directly associated with this temperature change but rather to some other changes in the tissues in association with the amount of energy absorbed [3,4]

2. Electromagnetic field effects

A wide spectrum of electromagnetic waves is today emitted by radar, communication equipment, mobile phone base stations, high voltage lines, radio and television transmitters, substations, and electrical equipment at home and work, in addition to many electrical systems in the environment [16]. The Global System for Mobile Communications (GSM, 850–900 MHz, and 1850–1990 MHz) is currently the most extensive system for mobile telecommunications worldwide [17,18]. The mobile phone models (1800 MHz −2200 MHz), laptops (1000 MHz–3600 MHz), and wireless networks in use today function with high frequency (2.45 GHz) microwave radiation [19].

This movement of ions causes deterioration in the ion channels on the membrane, biochemical changes in the membrane, and consequent impairment of all cellular functions [24].

 Increased body temperature is stabilized and alleviated by blood circulation. Although non-thermal effects do not raise the body temperature sufficiently to impair the structure of tissues, their effects can still be seen as an increase in free radical production in tissues [3]. EMFs, no matter where they occur in the frequency spectrum, are reported to cause a rise in levels of oxygen free radicals in an experimental environment in plants and humans

3. EMF-related oxidative stress and effects on tissue

The Fenton reaction is a catalytic process that converts hydrogen peroxide, a product of mitochondrial oxidative respiration, into a highly toxic hydroxyl free radical. Some studies have suggested that EMF is another mechanism through the Fenton reaction, suggesting that it promotes free radical activity in cells

Many studies have suggested that EMF may trigger the formation of reactive oxygen species in exposed cells in vitro [34,35,36,37] and in vivo [7,31,38]. The initial stage of the ROS production in the presence of RF is controlled by the NADPH oxidase enzyme located in the plasma membrane. Consequently, ROS activates matrix metalloproteases, thereby initiating intracellular signaling cascades to warn the nucleus of the presence of external stimulation.

Epidemiological studies have also suggested that oxidative damage to lipids in blood vessel walls may be a significant contributor to the development of atherosclerosis

Oxidative stress plays an important role in DNA damage process, general and specific gene expression, and cell apoptosis.

Excessive amounts of ROS in tissues may lead to necrosis, the death of neurons, and neuronal damage in brain tissue, as well as to neurological disorders such as Alzheimer's disease, spinal cord injury, multiple sclerosis, and epilepsy [70] (Fig. 2). Several studies have observed neuronal damage and cellular losses caused by exposure to EMF in many regions of the brain, including the cortex, basal ganglia, hippocampus, and cerebellum [71,72,73,74,75]

Rubin et al. noted that the pain level of headache may increase during exposure but decreased immediately when exposure ceased [77]

Oxidative damage in DNA occurs as a result of interaction between free radicals and DNA, with the addition of bases or abstractions of hydrogen atoms from sugar moiety. Modified nucleotides emerge as products of damage (8-OH-dG) when DNA is modified by the oxidative damage caused by reactive oxygen molecules.

4. The antioxidant defense system and EMF

Antioxidant defense systems have developed in organisms to control the formation of free radicals and to prevent the harmful effects of these molecules

[122]. These antioxidants reduce or impair the damage mechanism of ROS via their free radical scavenging activities

If these antioxidant defense mechanisms are impaired through exposure to an agent that causes the overproduction of ROS, including EMF. Antioxidants may not be sufficient or free radical formation may increase to such an extent that it overpowers the defense capabilities of antioxidants [10]. This is known as oxidative stress. EMFs can initiate various biochemical and physiological changes, including oxidative stress, in the systems of various species.

Generally, antioxidants have been divided into exogenous groups (carotene, C, and vitamin E), and endogenous groups (melatonin (MEL)), SOD, GSH-Px, CAT, including; protein (MEL), vitamins (vitamin C), trace elements (Mg, Se), complexes of a compound, hydrophilic (ascorbic acid, urate, flavonoids) and hydrophobic (β-carotene, α-tocopherol) substances, with direct impacts (SOD, CAT), and indirect effects (vitamin E). Substances with functions concerning the membrane (vitamin A and E, β-carotene), circulation (vitamin C, amino acids, and polyphenols), and cytosol (co-enzyme Q10) are classified as antioxidants [122,128].

4.1. Glutathione

Glutathione (GSH) is an endogenous antioxidant and an important cellular defense agent against oxidative damage. GSH reacts with the free radicals in the cell and reduces the entry of hydrogen peroxides [129].

GSH levels in tissues are often used as a marker for measuring radical damage.

In the oxidative stress process, levels of GSH decrease, while glutathione disulfide increases. In this case, the accumulation of hydrogen peroxide (H_2O_2) is scavenged by the effects of reductase and glutathione peroxidase (GSH-Px). GSH-Px is also an important enzyme, which prevents damage to phagocytic cells caused by free radicals. A decrease in GSH-Px activity leads to the accumulation of hydrogen peroxide and cell damage. GSH-Px also prevents the initiation of lipid peroxidation [65]. EMF emitted by cellular phones is known to be related to a decreased level of GSH in brain tissue and blood.

Awad and Hassan investigated the brains of rats exposed to 900-MHz EMF from mobile phones for 1 h/day for one week. They observed an increase in lipid peroxidation after exposure to mobile phones [131]. Aydın and Akar studied the effect of 900-MHz EMF for 2 h/day for 45 days on lymphoid organs in immature and mature rats. They reported that CAT and GPx activities decreased significantly compared to a control group.

The obtained results showed regulation of the activities of antioxidant enzymes such as CAT and GR, which protect against oxidative damage induced by EMF [133]. Sepehrimanesh et al. studied the effect of 900-MHz electromagnetic field (EMF) exposure on rat serum and testes antioxidant enzyme levels. They observed that after 30 days of exposure, both SOD and GPx activities decreased in the long-time EMF exposure group [134]. In the other study, RF-EMF exposure caused increased antioxidant stress response via an increase in CAT and GR activity, which lead to the generation of lipid and protein oxidative damage [135].

4.2. Catalase

CAT is a common enzyme present in organisms exposed to oxygen, such as vegetables, fruits, and animals. It catalyzes the reaction that degrades hydrogen peroxide to water and oxygen. It is a crucial enzyme in the protection of the cell against oxidative damage caused by ROS.

4.3. Superoxide dismutase

SOD is an enzyme that catalyzes the reaction in which the toxic superoxide (O_2-) radical is partitioned into molecular oxygen (O_2) or hydrogen peroxide (H_2O_2). Superoxide is generated as a byproduct as a result of the oxygen metabolism, leading to several types of damage to cells.

5. Antioxidants alleviate the potential risks of EMF exposure

When antioxidant supplementation is applied with EMF exposure, it improves the hydrophilic, lipophilic, and enzymatic antioxidant blood capacity and partially compensates for these changes [147,148]. Vitamin E (tocopherol) is one of the most important of such antioxidants. Compounds of vitamin E, including alpha, beta, gamma, and delta tocopherols, are soluble in lipid.

Vitamin B9 (folic acid and folate) is crucial for several functions in the human body, ranging from the production of nucleotides to homocysteine remethylation. In humans, folate is required for the body to make or repair DNA, and methylate DNA, in addition to its function as a cofactor in various biological reactions.

6. Conclusion
The biological effect of exposure to EMF is a subject of particular research interest. The results of the recent studies not only clearly demonstrate that EMF exposure triggers oxidative stress in various tissues, but also that it causes significant changes in

levels of blood antioxidant markers. Fatigue, headache, decreased learning ability, and cognitive impairment is among the symptoms caused by EMF. The human body should therefore be protected against exposure to EMF because of the risks this can entail.

- NCBI

Assessment of the Possible Health Effects of Ground Wave

Emergency Network.

6 Effects of Electromagnetic Fields on Organs and Tissues

Introduction

A large body of literature exists on the response of tissues to electromagnetic fields, primarily in the extremely-low-frequency (ELF) and microwave-frequency ranges. In general, the reported effects of radiofrequency (RF) radiation on tissue and organ systems have been attributed to thermal interactions, although the existence of non-thermal effects at low field intensities is still a subject of active investigation.

Nervous System

The effects of radiation on nervous tissues have been a subject of active investigation since changes in animal behavior and nerve electrical properties were first reported in the Soviet Union during the 1950s and 1960s.[1] RF radiation is reported to affect isolated nerve preparations, the central nervous system, brain chemistry and histology, and the blood-brain barrier. In studies with in vitro nerve preparations, changes have been observed in the firing rates of Aplysia neurons and the refractory period of isolated frog sciatic nerves exposed to 2.45-GHz microwaves at SAR values exceeding 5 W/kg.[2,3,4] Those effects were very likely associated with the heating of the nerve preparations, in that; much higher SAR values have not been found to produce changes in the electrical properties of isolated nerves when the temperature was controlled.[5,6] Studies on isolated heart preparations have provided evidence of bradycardia as a result of exposure to RF radiation at nonthermal power densities,[7] although some of the reported effects might have been artifacts caused by currents induced in the recording electrodes or by nonphysiological conditions in the bathing medium.[8,9,10] Several groups of investigators have reported that nonthermal levels of RF fields can alter Ca^{2+} binding to the surfaces of nerve cells in isolated brain hemispheres and neuroblastoma cells cultured in vitro (reviewed by the World Health Organization[11] and in Chapters 3 and 7 of this report). That phenomenon, however, is observed only when the RF field is amplitude-modulated at extremely low frequencies, the maximum effect occurs at a modulation frequency of 16 Hz. A similar effect has recently been reported in isolated frog hearts.[12] The importance of changes in Ca^{2+} binding on the functional properties of nerve cells has not been established, and there is no clear evidence that the reported effect of low-intensity, amplitude-modulated RF fields pose a substantial health risk.

A wide variety of changes in brain chemistry and structure have been reported after exposure of animals to high-intensity RF fields.[19] The changes include decreased concentrations of epinephrine, norepinephrine, dopamine, and 5-hydroxytryptamine; changes in the axonal structure; a decreased number of Purkinje cells; and structural alterations in the hypothalamic region. Those effects have generally been associated with RF intensities that produced substantial local heating in the brain.

Reactive oxygen species - British Pharmacological Society[3]

ROS are a group of small reactive molecules that play critical roles in the regulation of various cell functions and biological processes. In contrast, uncontrolled **overproduction of ROS** resulting from an imbalance of **ROS** generation and elimination leads to the development of vascular diseases[4]. Apr 11, 2017

Reactive oxygen species[5]

Major cellular sources of ROS in living non-photosynthetic cells. From a review by Novo and Parola, 2008.[1][2]

Reactive oxygen species (ROS) are chemically reactive chemical species containing oxygen.

---

[3] bpspubs.onlinelibrary.wiley.com › doi › pdf › bph

[4] https://en.wikipedia.org/wiki/Reactive_oxygen_species

[5] From Wikipedia, the free encyclopedia

Examples include peroxides, superoxide, hydroxyl radical, singlet oxygen,[3] and alpha-oxygen.

The reduction of molecular oxygen (O_2) produces superoxide ($•O_2^-$), which is the precursor of most other reactive oxygen species:[4]

$$O_2 + e^- \rightarrow •O_2^-$$

Dismutation of superoxide produces hydrogen peroxide (H_2O_2) :[4]

$$2H^+ + •O_2^- + •O_2^- \rightarrow H_2O_2 + O_2$$

Hydrogen peroxide in turn may be partially reduced, thus forming hydroxide ion and hydroxyl radical ($•OH$), or fully reduced to water:[4]

$$H_2O_2 + e^- \rightarrow HO^- + •OH$$
$$2H^+ + 2e^- + H_2O_2 \rightarrow 2H_2O$$

In a biological context, ROS are formed as a natural byproduct of the normal metabolism of oxygen and have important roles in cell signaling and homeostasis.[5] However, during times of environmental stress (e.g., UV or heat exposure), ROS levels can increase dramatically.[5] This may result in significant damage to cell structures. Cumulatively, this is known as oxidative stress. The production of ROS is strongly influenced by stress factor responses in plants, these factors that increase ROS production included rought, salinity, chilling, nutrient deficiency, metal toxicity, and UV B radiation. ROS are also generated by exogenous sources such as ionizing radiation.[6]

How does ROS damage cells?
Oxidative **damage**
In addition to energy, **reactive oxygen species** (**ROS**) with the potential to cause **cellular damage are** produced. **ROS can damage** lipid, DNA, RNA, and proteins, which, in theory, contributes to the physiology of aging. **ROS are** produced as a normal product of **cellular** metabolism.

Can our body combat free radicals[6]?

---

[6] https://www.google.com/search?sxsrf=ALeKk02Gk_-_42fQRuhr45HAQDm6ujm3Hw:1587178616137&q=Can+our+body+combat+free+radicals%3F&sa=X&ved=2ahUKEwjxg_CM_fDoAhWlgnIEHSueCDMQzmd6BAgLECM

What enzyme protects against free radicals?
Glutathione peroxidase (GPx) is an enzyme that is responsible for protecting cells from damage due to free radicals like hydrogen and lipid peroxides.

How are free radicals generated?
Oxidative stress occurs when an oxygen molecule splits into single atoms with unpaired electrons, which are called **free radicals**. ... Electrons like to be in pairs, so these atoms, called **free radicals**, scavenge the body to seek out other electrons so they can become a pair. This causes damage to cells, proteins, and DNA. May 27, 2016

How do you increase glutathione peroxidase[7]?
Below are 10 of the best ways to increase your glutathione levels naturally.

1. Consume Sulfur-Rich Foods. Share on Pinterest. ...
2. Increase Your Vitamin C Intake. ...
3. Add Selenium-Rich Foods to Your Diet. ...
4. Eat Foods Naturally Rich in Glutathione. ...
5. Supplement With Whey Protein. ...
6. Consider Milk Thistle. ...
7. Try Turmeric Extract. ...

---

[7] https://www.google.com/search?sxsrf=ALeKk02MVTIyMo-dPTYXXRoxR-SLV-In6A%3A1587310664795&ei=SHCcXuKOMImsytMPvNasqAg&q=Glutathione+peroxidase+%28GPx%29+foods&oq=Glutathione+peroxidase+%28GPx%29+foods&gs_lcp=CgZwc3ktYWIQAzoEC AAQRzoGCAAQFhAeOgUIABDNAjoFCCEQoAE6BQghEKsCOggIIR AWEB0QHlC7pwFYvtkBYKziAWgAcAJ4AIABwQGIAc8FkgEDMy 4zmAEAoAEBqgEHZ3dzLXdpeg&sclient=psy-ab&ved=0ahUKEwji0sqC6fToAhUJlnIEHTwrC4UQ4dUDCAw&uact=5

8. Get Enough Sleep.

What Are Free Radicals? | Live Science[8]

Oxidative stress can occur when there is an imbalance of free radicals and <u>antioxidants</u> in the body.

The body's cells produce free radicals during normal metabolic processes. However, cells also produce

---

[8] www.livescience.com › 54901-free-radicals

antioxidants that neutralize these free radicals. In general, the body is able to maintain a balance between antioxidants and free radicals[9].

Superoxide dismutase is an enzyme that helps break down potentially harmful oxygen molecules in cells, which might prevent damage to tissues. It is being researched to see if it can help conditions where oxygen molecules are believed to play a role in disease.

Intravenous superoxide dismutase as a protective agent to prevent impairment of lung function induced by high tidal volume ventilation

ROS are a group of small reactive molecules that play critical roles in the regulation of various cell functions and biological processes. ... In contrast, uncontrolled **overproduction of ROS** resulting from an imbalance of **ROS** generation and elimination leads to the development of vascular diseases.

How can I lower my Ros?

---

[9] https://www.medicalnewstoday.com/articles/324863#free-radicals

These mechanisms to counteract **ROS** production include the use of the Superoxide Dismutase (SOD) family, which catalyzes the initial reaction of O_2- to hydrogen peroxide (H_2O_2), a product that will eventually **reduce** to water through glutathione peroxidase and catalase.

How does ROS damage cells?
Oxidative **damage**
In addition to energy, **reactive oxygen species (ROS)** with the potential to cause **cellular damage are** produced. **ROS can damage** lipid, DNA, RNA, and proteins, which, in theory, contributes to the physiology of aging. **ROS are** produced as a normal product of **cellular** metabolism.

Intravenous superoxide dismutase is a protective agent to prevent impairment of lung function induced by high tidal volume ventilation.

THIS IS WHY PEOPLE DIE MORE FROM VENTILATORS!!!

Background

For more than half a century, positive-pressure mechanical ventilation has been regarded as an essential intervention in assisting patients with respiratory failure in the intensive care unit and

facilitating oxygenation in the operating room. On the other hand, evidence from patient studies indicates that mechanical ventilation is one of the primary factors leading to hospital-acquired lung injury,
Pulmonary oxidative stress and lung inflammation had been implicated in the pathogenesis of ventilator-associated pulmonary dysfunction and lung injury [10, 15, 60, 68]. Overinflating alveoli and repeated stretching of lung tissues can produce reactive oxygen species (ROS), and diminish prostanoid synthesis promoting redox imbalance and cyclooxygenase induction, and inflammatory responses [68]. Also, the formation of ROS disrupts the regulation of nitric oxide synthase (NOS) causing nitrotyrosine accumulation, irregular tracheal mucus secretion, and increased airway resistance [63

Superoxide dismutase (SOD) is an important antioxidant, active in endothelial cells, cytoplasm, and mitochondrial intermembrane matrix [57]. It protects cells against superoxide damage by catalyzing the dismutation of superoxide radicals into molecular oxygen and hydrogen peroxide, [50, 57] and thus inhibits peroxynitrite-mediated oxidative protein modification and cell membrane lipid peroxidation [27]. Moreover, SOD can facilitate vascular function, increasing nitric oxide (NO) bioavailability through competing with NO for superoxide anions [31]. SOD was also shown to inhibit neutrophil-mediated inflammation by regulating neutrophil apoptosis [85]. Despite all the benefits and no major side effects, the therapeutic efficacy of SOD treatment on tissue damage, in general, has been limited by its short circulatory half-life and low transcapillary permeability, due to its relatively large molecular size (molecular weight ~ 32 kDa) [84]. On the other hand, intravenous administration of Cu/Zn SOD has been demonstrated to be effective against hyperoxia-induced lung injury [53][10]

---

[10] https://www.ncbi.nlm.nih.gov/pmc/articles/PMC5530466/

To Your Health: Is SOD available in food or do I need to get it[11]?

1. https://webcache.googleusercontent.com/search?q=cache:2ozPhlu4zuQJ:https://www.austinchronicle.com/columns/2006-03-24/349701/+&cd=4&hl=en&ct=clnk&gl=us

These foods that are rich sources of SOD, such as broccoli, cabbage, or barley grass, are also good sources of the minerals (zinc, copper, and manganese) that our bodies use to make our SOD, and this may explain the slight boost in blood SOD from supplements[12].

---

[11] www.austinchronicle.com

[12] https://www.google.com/search?sxsrf=ALeKk03IunnJcggdZwxgovtehc-vtzuuZw%3A1587177885619&source=hp&ei=nWmaXvDjIsyb_Qb61Ih4&q=Superoxide+dismutase+in+food&oq=Superoxide+dismutase+in+food&gs_lcp=CgZwc3ktYWIQAzICCAAyBggAEBYQHjIFCAAQzQIyBQgAEM0CMgUIABDNAjIFCAAQzQI6BwgjEOoCECc6BAgjECc6BAgAEEM6BwgAEBQQhwJQzSFYuEZg0lBoAnAAeACAAdoDiAHUCJIBBTguNC0xmAEAoAECoAEBqgEHZ3dzLXdpcGVyABCg&sclient=psy-ab&ved=0ahUKEwiwpsKw-vDoAhXMTd8KHXoqAg8Q4dUDCAk&uact=5

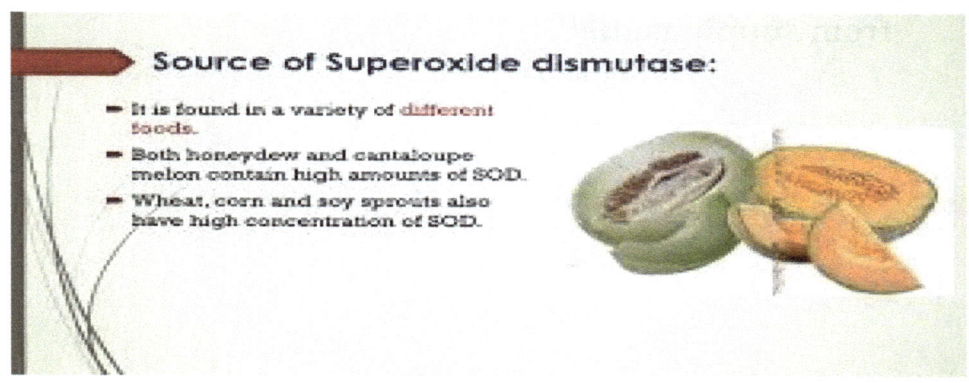

superoxide dismutase supplement

ROS Function in Redox Signaling and Oxidative Stress

Abstract

Oxidative stress refers to elevated intracellular levels of reactive oxygen species (ROS) that cause damage to lipids, proteins, and DNA.

Introduction

Reactive oxygen species (ROS) are byproducts of aerobic metabolism. ROS include the superoxide anion (O_2^-), hydrogen peroxide (H_2O_2), and hydroxyl radicals ($OH^.$), all of which have inherent chemical properties that confer reactivity to different biological targets. ROS is often associated with the principle of oxidative stress which suggests ROS induces pathology by damaging lipids, proteins, and DNA [1].

H_2O_2 is generated from superoxide produced by mitochondria and NADPH oxidases [8, 9]. Superoxide forms from the one-electron reduction of molecular oxygen, (O_2) within the cell, and is rapidly converted by superoxide dismutases 1 and 2 (SOD 1 and 2) into H_2O_2.

Thus, the accumulation of superoxide is more associated with oxidative stress than redox signaling.

How can you protect your home from EMF?
My Solutions for Lowering Your EMF Pollution Exposure
Buy An EMF Protection Cell Phone Case.
1. Avoid Body Contact with Your Cell Phone and Computer.
2. Get Grounded.
3. Use Healing Crystals.
4. Create A Low EMF Sanctuary.
5. Remove Smart Meters.
6. Spend More Time with People and In Nature.

ROS Function in Redox Signaling and Oxidative Stress

Oxidative stress refers to elevated intracellular levels of reactive oxygen species (ROS) that cause damage to lipids, proteins, and DNA.

Reactive oxygen species (ROS) are byproducts of aerobic metabolism. ROS include the superoxide anion (O_2^-), hydrogen peroxide (H_2O_2), and hydroxyl radicals (OH˙), all of which have inherent chemical properties that confer reactivity to different biological targets. ROS is often associated with the principle of oxidative stress which suggests ROS induces pathology by damaging lipids, proteins, and DNA [1].

H_2O_2 is generated from superoxide produced by mitochondria and NADPH oxidases [8, 9].

Superoxide forms from the one-electron reduction of molecular oxygen (O_2) and, within the cell, is rapidly converted by superoxide dismutases 1 and 2 (SOD 1 and 2) into H_2O_2.

How does oxidative stress affect the body?

<u>What is it?</u> Oxidative stress is an imbalance of free radicals and antioxidants in the body, which can lead to cell and tissue damage.

How do you detox your body from radiation?
Eat antioxidant-rich foods of every color, especially cherries, blueberries, pomegranates, yams, and sweet potatoes. The
variety of antioxidants found in these foods helps your body to mop up free radicals and toxins. Drink six to eight 8-ounce glasses of filtered water every day to flush and hydrate your system.

Peroxynitrite (sometimes called peroxynitrite) is an ion with the formula $ONOO^-$. It is an unstable structural isomer of nitrate, NO^-_3. Although its conjugate acid peroxynitrous acid is highly reactive, **peroxynitrite** is stable in basic solutions.

What is peroxynitrite damage?
Peroxynitrite is a powerful oxidant exhibiting a wide array of tissue-**damaging** effects, including lipid peroxidation, inactivation of enzymes and ion channels via protein oxidation and nitration, and inhibition of mitochondrial respiration (Virag et al., 2003).

Peroxynitrite is a potent cytotoxic chemical that is formed naturally in the body by the interaction of nitric oxide and superoxide radicals (which result from EMF exposure) ([17](), [18]())

8. Eat these spices and take a magnesium supplement

Spices rich in phenolics, including cinnamon, turmeric, ginger, cloves, and rosemary are shown in research to help protect as well as repair damage from EMF due to their protective capacity against peroxynitrites.

Also, since magnesium is a natural calcium channel blocker, it helps reduce the effects of EMF on your VGCCs. As a result, optimizing your magnesium level may help decrease damage from EMFs.

Can our body combat free radicals[13]?

What enzyme protects against free radicals?
Glutathione peroxidase (GPx) is an enzyme that is responsible for protecting cells from damage due to free radicals like hydrogen and lipid peroxides.

What characterizes a free radical?
A **free radical** is any atom or molecule that has a single unpaired electron in an outer shell. ... For most biological structures, **free radical** damage is closely associated with oxidative damage. Antioxidants are reducing agents, and limit oxidative damage to biological structures by passivating them from **free radicals**.

The free-radical theory of aging[14]

Abnormally high concentrations of **free radicals** in the body can be **caused** by exposure to ionizing radiation and other environmental toxins. Feb 6, 2017

---

[13] https://www.google.com/search?sxsrf=ALeKk02Gk_-_42fQRuhr45HAQDm6ujm3Hw:1587178616137&q=Can+our+body+combat+free+radicals%3F&sa=X&ved=2ahUKEwjxg_CM_fDoAhWlgnIEHSueCDMQzmd6BAgLECM

[14] en.wikipedia.org › wiki › Free-radical_theory_of_aging

Antioxidants and Cancer Prevention - National Cancer Institute[15]

Superoxide dismutase 1 acts as a nuclear transcription factor to regulate oxidative stress resistance[16]

Chi Kwan Tsang,1,3 Yuan Liu,1,2 Janice Thomas,1,3 Yanjie Zhang,1,3 and X. F. Steven Zheng[1,3,*]

Drug Treatment and Indirect Immunofluorescence Microscopy

Exponentially growing yeast cells were treated with oxidative agents

Associated Data

Supplementary Materials

Summary

Superoxide dismutase 1 (Sod1) has been known for nearly half a century for the catalysis of superoxide to hydrogen peroxide. Here

---

[15] www.cancer.gov › risk › diet › antioxidants-fact-shee

[16] https://www.ncbi.nlm.nih.gov/pmc/articles/PMC4678626/

What radio frequency is harmful to humans?

The most restrictive limits on whole-body exposure are in the frequency range of 30-300 **MHz** where the human body absorbs RF energy most efficiently when the whole body is exposed.

What frequency is dangerous?

The most restrictive limits on whole-body exposure are in the **frequency** range of 30-300 MHz where the human body absorbs RF energy most efficiently when the whole body is exposed.

Free radicals from radiation
Exposure of cells to ionizing **radiation** leads to a **free radical** formation that damages both DNA and the cytoplasmic organelles and endoplasmic reticulum. High linear energy transfer (LET) **radiation** can directly damage DNA strands without affecting the activity of **free radicals**.

Radiation damage and radioprotectants: new concepts in the.[17]

Biological Effects of Power Frequency Electric and Magnetic Fields May 1989 NTIS order #PB89-209985

Intravenous superoxide dismutase as a protective agent to prevent impairment of lung function induced by high tidal volume ventilation18
Background
Positive-pressure mechanical ventilation is essential in assisting patients with respiratory failure in the intensive care unit and facilitating oxygenation in the operating room. However, it was also recognized as a primary factor leading to hospital-acquired pulmonary dysfunction, in which pulmonary oxidative stress and lung inflammation had been known to play important roles. Cu/Zn superoxide dismutase (SOD) is an important antioxidant and

---

[17] https://www.google.com/search?sxsrf=ALeKk01YloXPf2R5-lR4_fze6qTKY9Po3g%3A1587311102408&ei=_nGcXpe8GJWwytMPsMW9sA8&q=blocking+radiation+free+radicals&oq=blocking+radiation+free+radicals&gs_lcp=CgZwc3ktYWIQAzoECAAQRzoHCCMQsAIQJzoECCEQClD1iwFYi5wBYJ6jAWgAcAJ4AIABVIgBjQaSAQIxMJgBAKABAaoBB2d3cy13aXo&sclient=psy-ab&ved=0ahUKEwiXs6DT6vToAhUVmHIEHbBiD_YQ4dUDCAw&uact=5

18 https://www.ncbi.nlm.nih.gov/pmc/articles/PMC5530466/

possesses an anti-inflammatory capacity. In this study, we aimed to study the efficacy of Cu/Zn SOD, administered intravenously during high tidal volume (HTV) ventilation, to prevent impairment of lung function.

Results

Five hours of LTV ventilation did not induce a major change in lung function, whereas 5 h of HTV ventilation, induced apparent combined restrictive and obstructive lung disorder, together with increased pulmonary oxidative stress, decreased anti-oxidative activity, and increased lung inflammation ($P < 0.05$). HTV ventilation also decreased SP-A and SP-D expression and suppressed serum NO levels during the time course of ventilation. Cu/Zn SOD administered intravenously during HTV ventilation effectively reversed associated pulmonary oxidative stress and lung inflammation ($P < 0.05$); moreover, it preserved SP-A and SP-D expressions in the lung and increased serum nitric oxide (NO) levels, enhancing vascular NO bioavailability.

Conclusions

HTV ventilation can induce combined restrictive and obstructive lung disorders. Intravenous administration of Cu/Zn SOD during HTV ventilation can prevent lung function impairment and lung injury via reducing pulmonary oxidative stress and lung inflammation, preserving pulmonary surfactant expression, and enhancing vascular NO bioavailability.

On the other hand, evidence from patient studies indicates that mechanical ventilation is one of the primary factors leading to hospital-acquired lung injury, and patients with burn injury, trauma, or pre-existing respiratory diseases are particularly at high risk [40]. A recent survey of patients having cardiac surgery revealed that though most patients do not have signs of pulmonary dysfunction or lung injury before the surgery, some eventually develop perioperative lung injury [18]. Though the exact mechanism responsible is uncertain, higher tidal volume employed commonly to reduce risks of hypoxemia and pulmonary atelectasis is thought to play a critical role [38].

Pulmonary oxidative stress and lung inflammation had been implicated in the pathogenesis of ventilator-associated pulmonary dysfunction and lung injury [10, 15, 60, 68]. Overinflating alveoli and repeated stretching of lung tissues can produce reactive oxygen species (ROS), and diminish prostanoid synthesis promoting redox imbalance and cyclooxygenase induction, and inflammatory responses [68]. Also, the formation of ROS disrupts the regulation of nitric oxide synthase (NOS) causing nitrotyrosine accumulation, irregular tracheal mucus secretion, and increased airway resistance [63]. In addition, stretching lung tissues directly alters the metabolism and secretion of pulmonary surfactant proteins (SPs) that mediate alveolar surface tension and lung compliance, while surfactant protein-A (SP-A) and D (SP-D) augment pulmonary immune defense mechanisms and inhibit endogenous lipid peroxidation [4]. Moreover, excessive lung stretch activates nuclear factor-κB (NF-κB) that mediates the production and release of proinflammatory cytokines and chemokines that, in turn, promote adhesion molecule expression [28] and facilitate inflammatory cell infiltration in the lung [34]. For over two decades, low tidal volume ventilation has been proposed as a protective strategy;

Superoxide dismutase (SOD) is an important antioxidant, active in endothelial cells, cytoplasm, and mitochondrial intermembrane matrix [57]. It protects cells against superoxide damage through catalyzing the dismutation of superoxide radicals into molecular oxygen and hydrogen peroxide [50, 57] and thus inhibits peroxynitrite-mediated oxidative protein modification and cell membrane lipid peroxidation [27]. Moreover, SOD can facilitate vascular function, increasing nitric oxide (NO) bioavailability through competing with NO for superoxide anions [31]. SOD was also shown to inhibit neutrophil-mediated inflammation by regulating neutrophil apoptosis [85]. Despite all the benefits and no major side effects, the therapeutic efficacy of SOD treatment on tissue damage, in general, has been limited by its short circulatory half-life and low transcapillary permeability, due to its relatively large molecular size (molecular weight ~ 32 kDa) [84].

Cu/Zn SOD mediates pulmonary vascular resistance and airway smooth muscle relaxation through increasing vascular nitric oxide (NO) bioavailability while reducing iNOS expression

<u>Nitric oxide regulates basal systemic and pulmonary vascular resistance in healthy humans.</u>

Search Results
Featured snippet from the web[19]

First of all, to answer your question: Yes, **Copper**, usually in the form of a **copper** mesh, will shield against most wavelength radiofrequency radiation and other **EMF** radiation. **Copper** is highly effective at blocking, or shielding, radiofrequency radiation because it absorbs radio and magnetic waves. Feb 1, 2018

Does Copper Block EMF Radiation? - EMF Academy[20]

19

https://www.google.com/search?q=copper+to+block+emf&sxsrf=ALeKk01AaMXaPJ34k1cbFtyEm07GU2xgCw:1587311740726&tbm=isch&source=iu&ictx=1&fir=iscgvc2KPTBbwM%3A%2C5AGG-Ak-VX4_uM%2C_&vet=1&usg=AI4_-kQoMd7c5AsFCFGsSy1J92bSMui5uw&sa=X&ved=2ahUKEwiKltCD7fToAhUIUt8KHcmCAAMQ9QEwAHoECAQQAw - imgrc=iscgvc2KPTBbwM:

20

https://www.google.com/search?sxsrf=ALeKk01yjysghI4_D3HGVrcByJ0N0nhosg%3A1587311731132&source=hp&ei=c3ScXvzcBYHt_Qbm0ZGIAw&q=copper+to+block+emf&oq=copper+to+block+emf&gs_lcp=CgZwc3ktYWIQAzICCAAyBQgAEM0CMgUIABDNAjIFCAAQzQIyBQgAEM0COgcIIxDqAhAnOgQIIxAnOgUIABCRAjoFCAAQgwE6BAgAEEM6BggAEAoQQzoECAAQCjoGCAAQFhAeOggIABAWEAoQHlDYDVjGPGC8QmgCcAB4AIABkQWIAagSkgEKMTQuMy4xLjUtMZgBAKABAaoBB2d3cy13aXqwAQo&sclient=psy-ab&ved=0ahUKEwi84oT_7PToAhWBdt8KHeZoBDEQ4dUDCAk&uact=5
https://webcache.googleusercontent.com/search?q=cache:5AGG-Ak-VX4J:https://emfacademy.com/copper-block-emf-radiation/+&cd=3&hl=en&ct=clnk&gl=us

47

1.

MY CONCLUSION
Increased EMF leads to Increase ROS; causes cell damage, leads to oxidative stress, produces H2O2, Leads to NO OXYGEN, THEN DEATH (AXPHYSIATION).
Using a ventilator further increases ROS, causing even more damage, H2O2, oxidative stress, and then death.

KGK 4/18/2020

4/20/2020 – For the Record: I am not stating that the pandemic is the effect of radiation. I am stating what God told me and where He led me. The studies were not over a long period. It took just

several hours of information just presenting itself right in from me, and I documented it. I am a professional nurse in the health care sector for almost 30 years and I am A Child of GOD. I would love it if this pandemic disappears. I cannot explain from where the image of this virus came (Is it a damaged cell?) or how is it transmitted (contagious)? Is radiation transferable? when I worked in the nuclear stress lab; radiation spills, patients injected with an isotope were radioactive, and radiation requires special handling. Patients traveling after an isotope injection (test to check the heart–stress test), are given documents to show and inform airport authorities that they have been injected with a radioactive substance that can trigger airport-sensitive alarms.

I hope it is some virus from an animal or lab... I think that would have been contained by now. Unless it s just that contagious and deadly. Nevertheless, WHO is loaded with smart people.

If it is a virus, it should go away with time. We may definitely require vaccination of some sort, for human flesh to survive outdoors.

If it is the effect of high radioactive waves, I pray the genius involved is prepared for what is ignited. However, I don t think so... Does radiation, when turned on emit rather heavy deadly waves to get the process started? Or is it the cause of constant emission... If so, we are in trouble. To what level of sacrifice do we give for more knowledge/power??? Or is it, Greed?? For once, man may finally have to choose either to turn off this event that is causing higher frequency waves than we already have, ... Or IT IS THE ONLY HUMAN RIGHT DECISION TO MAKE... GO TO GOD FOR ANSWERS!

CHAPTER TWO

Follow up 2021

8/12/2021 - FOLLOW UP FAST, TO FAST 1/2020

We are still in the phase of the "pandemic" and another fast was abruptly requested and required by God.

In the final week of February 2020, God clearly showed me a vision of two separate numbers "2's" (2 2).

It was clear that they represented two separate events, and I believe it to be related to "covid."

I reasoned with God, and before now, He told me to go food shopping and to ensure that my home was well stored with food, toiletries, etc. He told me to max my credit cards to buy necessary items including (medicines, sanitary items, lotions, everything, etc.). I DID! I also instructed everyone within my circle. Of course, the information was too important to bear. So, I told my church members exactly what God instructed; regarding shopping and being prepared because something is coming. They believed Not... It's ok... I realized that they could not see. I am to be passionate, caring, and to minister.

Well, according to the first image "2," it took EXACTLY TWO WEEKS (from the day of the revelation) FOR THE HAVOC AND CHAOS TO START. ITEMS WENT MISSING FROM STORES, due to high demand (toiletries, beverages, etc.), and Covid quickly spreading and becoming more deadly. I reasoned with God about the second number "2" and I thanked him for the pre-warning to be prepared... God is EXACT!

In reasoning with God regarding the second vision of the number "2," I said, "God, does that second "2" mean that covid will end in two months?" I felt His No, immediately...
I said, "God, is it two years?" I instantly felt His affirmation in my heart. I continued to reason with Him, I said, "Does the "2" represent two hundred years? I laughed at myself and said, "Then it would not make sense to tell me." I will not be here in 200 years. My heart went back to hearing two years and standing by what the Father said. This puts us in the final week of 2/2022.

I was eager to hear more from God and earnestly willing to have Him show me the pieces.

By January 2021, I did another 21-days prayer and fasting, but God did not show me anything regarding " Covid "per se. Rather, He revealed to me matters concerning, the overall reason; God vs devil, and the prophetical time that we are living in. I searched to get the spiritual connection because I knew in time, He will reveal things to me.
God revealed things about ministry and my role in doing His work. Consequently, He gave me the necessary information needed to proceed. Of course, during all this time, I was reasoning with the Father and He had shown me so many things. I also ASKED SO MANY questions concerning my task. I was ready to do what was necessary to please God.

By the end of July 2021. God said, "You are going to fast and pray for 21 days in August. I hadn't much time to prepare at all, but I accepted it as the best way! Thank God.

My 21 Days Prayer and Fasting of August 2021 Post Documentation.

Today is 1/28/2022, and I have decided to gather all the information again, from my place of fasting and publish it.
May God be with His children. We all have the DNA of GOD, which is GOD THE FATHER, SON, HOLY SPIRIT. TRINITY.
Matthew 11:15
15 He that hath ears to hear, let him hear. (KJV)

AUGUST 2021 FASTING and PRAYERS

Day 1 - Day 7, I was focused on deep spiritual insight. On day 7, I developed a small head sniffle, regardless, I kept studying, worshipping, clinging, and waiting on God

Day -10, I was feeling weird chest and stomach uneasiness. It was more like spiritual sickness as if something was deeply wrong.

Day - 12, Tower of Babel - LHC (large hadron collider) off Switzerland

Day - 13, Higgs Boson

Day - 14, muons / mrna ribonucleic acid

Day - 15, USA Fermilab (located off Chicago was located in LI, NY) something happened. MUON

Day - 16, Discovery today: new particle discovered at LHC

Day - 17, Human antenna mRNA targets - magnetic field, PULLS MUON out of the atmosphere (the god particle "muons" is found in the atmosphere).

Day - 18, smh

Day - 19, Only GOD the FATHER, SON, and HOLY SPIRIT. The Nation of Father Abraham.

Those were the recorded events during my 21 days of fasting and prayers in August 2021. Of course, there was a lot more research concerning the connection between the events. However, I will not list it all here. God showed me the names, how, why, and where; as to exactly what's going on regarding "Covid," and the prophetic connection.
Scientists from inception had been tampering with God's creation. They have opened the "Pandora's box" though, they know what that means. REPENT.

The Great Controversy is Real. We all knew it, but the pieces are to be revealed... If we STAND and ASK!
The revelation is for those who seek and those willing to see. The instruction was given by God to preach to His people. Get your life together, surrender to God, resist the devil, and he will flee from you.

After the 12 days of fasting and prayers in August 2021, my spirit was blown. It became overwhelming for me, especially after seeing the blindness or blind eye of the world. I saw the anger and tension brewing. The most interesting thing God alerted me to was the natural disasters. The earth is shaking terribly. Something is coming closer and closer to where I am. The earthquakes, volcanoes, tornadoes, floods, mudslides, and so many catastrophes are not just natural occurrences. The time is at hand, it will be best that we take heed.

In September 2021, I was recommended to listen to Pastor Cameron Bowen from the Character-Building Prayer Line. My friend said that I speak like him and I could learn from him. It was indeed a blessing. He opened my mind to the connection between Afghanistan and the Spiritual covenant, since Abraham. I was open to learning more about Abraham's other children.

There are some in other folds however that need to hear Jesus. They are willing and open. Some suffer many persecutions by just following Christ.

NOTHING IS A SURPRISE TO GOD!

Pastor Cameron Bowen, died several weeks after, I started listening to him.

All this information was too much to keep inside me. So, I asked God, what do I do with this information? ... It's so heavy.... I felt the need to be careful and protect myself, so I did not share much except with a friend. Lol, I knew it was a lot for her to process, but she had an open ear and mind.... I still didn't feel that I had shared enough regarding this information. I Didn't know who to trust, who would understand, or someone who sees. (Wow)

God directed me to Revelation 13: 15-17

15 And he had power to give life unto the image of the beast, that the image of the beast should both speak, and cause that as many as would not worship the image of the beast should be killed. (KJV)

 I GOT IT - That "muon" was the 3rd particle to the devil's fake replicated DNA of what he (satan) thinks is the match to God's DNA.... (They already had two particles, that the devil gave them and are aiming to

get the third particle - smart computers - guess whose? Guess whose software would be used for those computers? Guess who developed the code to get muons?)
The devil wants to be worshipped.

10/8/2021, "SESAME" - other lab facilities, there are more. (Noted documentation)

On a Sabbath evening, on October 16th, 2021, I was opening YouTube, and a bright idea came to me.
(I thought it was my idea), I said, "God, look some people are doing live shows/events/posts right now. I am going to blast their live chat with some of the information you showed me. If they are your children, they will see and take action." I blasted three live happenings on YouTube. The first two were sabbath events with panels of speakers, I wrote, "Help, Help. Some bad things are happening in the world, and some bad people are behind them. Please google muons, law case to stop accelerators in LHR and other labs,"
Revelation 13:17, and much more. I was adamant that someone would see and look further.

I then saw my third and final live show that I would blast their live chat.
(I did not want to overdo it and draw attention to myself. Forgive me, God.)

It was a Jamaican pastor. He was talking to an audience, seems like they were in front of him. I could not see them; the camera was on him. He was talking to the audience while the camera was on him and you can clearly see him responding to a computer, to the side of the camera. He would glimpse at the computer and respond, from to time, and looked toward members in front of him. I even saw him responding to someone online, telling them to come. I didn't listen to what he was saying in-depth, he just looked like a talkative that will take action. I was so happy because I knew he saw what I said in his chat. When I posted my revelation, he looked at the chat, he did a very small nod, paused, then refocused on whatever he was talking about.

I felt that I was somewhat incognito and someone will open their mouth and take the action. I was happy, I told him the information I put on the previous two live posts that there are a lot of bad people in the world.

A few minutes later, the live post ended. You could see my posts in the chat. It was a lot and easy to spot. I thought nothing much. Maybe the church was over and I got the last few minutes before they ended the program. I shared a lot of information in the chat, and hoped THEY WILL SEE IT and take action,

That same week, a few days later, precisely Thursday, October 21st, 2021, my church sister gifted with dreaming, told me she had a dream. She saw a lot of blood in a church. By the evening, she sent me pictures of dead bloody naked bodies on a floor in a church in Jamaica W.I. Apparently, some sort of sacrificial event took place.

That following Sabbath evening, being October 23rd, I decided to go online to see what happened at that Church in Jamaica. To my surprise, it was the same preacher that I made my post in his chat, just a few days before. His name was Kevin Smith. (He died a few days later in a car accident in Jamaica while traveling in police custody on October 25th.)

Apparently, he told his members to gather in the church for 3 days (he called the church; The Ark). It started on a Friday. He told his members that there is a flood coming (which probably is), but they are to get into the "ark" to be safe. I made my post on Saturday the following day. But his plan was already in motion.
It wasn't my bright idea to post on his live chat, It Was God's insight.). My message was saying REPENT!!!!!!
Sadly, on THE 3RD DAY, A DAY AFTER MY POST, THOSE LIVES WERE "sacrificed ".... mercy.

Devil is a liar....

I was totally shocked at this time. God showed me even more, about the fact that some people already have sold out to the beast... I felt very sad.

PROPHECY MUST BE FULFILLED.

In December 2021, the UN reveals a new statue ("a peace guardian image" that resembles a beast described in Daniel and Revelation). coincidence? No…. mercy…. someone is bragging…

NEXT: REVELATION 13: 15….

Summary: It took centuries for what is now here and done, to have been done. It is written…. "That system will be enforced to the limit. Only those who STAND will see God……"

P.S- the metaverse is funded by muons and a lot of other high technology. (The greatest man particle given by the devil) to greedy men. STOP PLAYING GOD.
WE WORSHIP ONE KING; OUR LORD AND SAVIOR, GOD, JESUS, AND HOLY SPIRIT.
God will seal all His people. HAVE FAITH! After reasoning again with God, I highly believe that covid will mysteriously disappear around February 2022.
I believe that the second image 2, which I saw on 2/2020, stands for two years. Maybe exactly two, our God is exact!!!
That means Revelation 13:15 is next. READ!!!

In January 2022 - I got some mind comfort. God reminded me that, "GOD'S GOT IT" (He's got it).

My job is to keep seeking the kingdom, pray, and share this gospel. God is Great and He is coming for His children. Will You Be Ready?

Luke 19:13
13 And he called his ten servants, and delivered them ten pounds, and said unto them, Occupy till I come. (KJV)

KGK

CHAPTER THREE

Tribulation

3/13/2022

TRIBULATION - TRIBULATION HAS BEGUN.

God once again instructed me to document this. He wants me to declare a time.

The final seven (7) year tribulation is the time when God finishes judging Israel. Humanity's decadence and depravity will reach their fullness with God judging accordingly. A time to finish the transgression, to put an end to sin, to atone for wickedness, to bring everlasting righteousness, to seal up vision and prophesy, and to account for the holiest.[21]

Daniel 9:24-27

24 Seventy weeks are determined upon thy people and upon thy holy city, to finish the transgression, and to make an end of sins, and to make reconciliation for iniquity, and to bring in everlasting righteousness, and to seal up the vision and prophecy, and to anoint the most Holy.

25 Know therefore and understand, that from the going forth of the commandment to restore and to build Jerusalem unto the Messiah the Prince shall be seven weeks, and threescore and two weeks: the

---

[21] Chapter 16 *"Close of Probation" Last Day Events* by EGW

street shall be built again, and the wall, even in troublous times.

26 And after threescore and two weeks shall Messiah be cut off, but not for himself: and the people of the prince that shall come shall destroy the city and the sanctuary; and the end thereof shall be with a flood, and unto the end of the war desolations are determined.

27 And he shall confirm the covenant with many for one week: and in the midst of the week he shall cause the sacrifice and the oblation to cease, and for the overspreading of abominations he shall make it desolate, even until the consummation, and that determined shall be poured upon the desolate. (KJV)

In addition to previous documentation:
On November 16th, 2021 - the UN reveals a "peace guardian" at the UN headquarters in NYC.
I believe it to be a direct statement that the beast is here. God directed me to Revelation 13:15…

Revelation 13:15
15 And he had power to give life unto the image of the beast, that the image of the beast should both speak, and cause that as many as would not worship the image of the beast should be killed. (KJV)

NOTE: The two YEARS of COVID (PLAGUE) according to God's revelation have elapsed. The virus, in fact, is decreasing. Rumors have that more variants are sprouting, while the vaccine is still been sent out. Hallelujah, some mandates have been lifted.

Even though covid is declining, mankind is not going to stop its mischief. That is why they will not be able to explain covid (the plague) and things to come. This is spiritual. Man has their conflict; however, this is between God and the devil, NOT MAN!

Man's time for judgment is near.

In 2020, in the final week of February, God showed me a vision of two separate numbers 2 and 2. (2 2) ... He said, "In two weeks, covid will hit humanity and create chaos all around.", He then said, "there will be two years to plague in the land." It is now two years and two weeks since the revelation of the vision in February 2020.

For the past three months, God has brought to my attention that the earth is changing and getting violent faster. I have seen increased earthquakes, mudslides, tornadoes, rocks falling, volcanoes, animals dying, a lot of other weird and extreme disasters happening, violence, and more. The space between one tragic event to the other is shorter. Like birth pains.

Messages to Have food at home, cash on hand were given. I was not sure exactly when and what is going to occur... We just know that the world is in chaos and anything, (even war), can happen. (Rice, canned goods, sugar, flour, oil, etc.), and constant talks of removing money from banks.

REMEMBER: the god particle "muons" ... Well, everyone has power and is ready to flex their powers. The scene is set. Christ is coming back for His children. Things of old, will face their promised judgment, says the Lord.

PRAY FOR MERCY AND GRACE. PRAY FOR FORGIVENESS.
What have people done?

February 2022 - Two years since the Vision of "2's" in 2/2020. Covid has declined. I told the church prayer line what God has said, however, I will pinpoint that it took almost two weeks into March 2020 for covid to cause chaos all around. I am continually bringing to the attention of people, earth's catastrophes; what is occurring presently, and what God has said regarding this plague and what is next. (Revelation 13: 15). I told everyone that the next two weeks are not going to be easy. There is something with mankind.

RUSSIA AND UKRAINE TENSION INCREASING, INVASION, SHELLING, WAR CRIMES, SANCTIONS, NUCLEAR THREATS, ETC.

On the third week of February 2022, there was an uneasiness in my chest down to my abdomen... I knew something was not right. I did not trust mankind, and I was being careful of earth's catastrophes. I took it to the Lord in Prayers.

On February 2/21/2022, after my 5 am prayer line, God said: Last Days Events. He said I am to discuss the "Last Days Events" with everyone. He pointed to:

Thessalonians 5 :3

"For when they shall say, Peace and safety; then sudden destruction cometh upon them, as travail upon a woman with child; and they shall not escape."

(KJV)

God instructed us to prepare, and 1 Thessalonians 5, is our motto.

I sat for the rest of the week in prayer with God regarding this, Peace and safety, then sudden destruction... He also directed me to read: Chapter 16 of the *Last Days Events* by EGW.

On 2/25/2022, God showed me what "sudden destruction meant."

MERCY* MERCY* MERCY*

I saw the vision clearly and He wants me to understand the connection. All roads lead to the papacy. We are in the last days and the prophesy that must take place. This is about God and the devil. The devil's plan is to be worshipped and captivate the minds of God's children. Bringing great deceptions to the world and church. This is about the 7-year tribulations leading to the final conflict and our Christ's return. Yeah!

Here is the Vision: The scene/ stage is set, for nations to be pulled into war. There is nothing they can do about it. When the United States is involved, the war officially starts. Once one Russian jet is bombed by the USA, it becomes too late… and vice versa. Everyone will be pulled in; China, Taiwan, Iran, and everyone.

Man has their reasons (flesh and worldly reasons) they think they are fighting, but it's already set to occur. The happenings of this time are Spiritual. They are the events that must occur before Christ's return.
It must occur in order for anti-Christ to position and enforce the mark of beast/mandates/no buy or sell etc. (satan wants to be worshipped)

Ezekiel 38:4
4 And I will turn thee back, and put hooks into thy jaws, and I will bring thee forth, and all thine army, horses and horsemen, all of them clothed with all sorts of armour, even a great company with bucklers and shields, all of them handling swords: (KJV)

It's decision time, and if you have not made up your mind on whose side you are on, a choice is then made for you.

Matthew 11:15 King James Version
15 He that hath ears to hear, let him hear. (KJV)

On 03/5/2022, on a sabbath evening, I was reasoning with my Lord. God showed me; that the decision **MUST BE** made by the **church, the world, and all peoples; me included,** to listen to Him and build Knight Life Entertainment to help people.

In the second week of March (7th-11th) 2022, I experienced a lot of muscle pain.

On 3/11/2022, I received the message to document. I then had to go into prayer and worship. I wanted the Sabbath to flow so that I can hear from God as to what to document.

On March 12th 2022, after spending some time with open ears, I heard…

God wanted me to document **the "tribulation" and that it had started or was about to start.** He led me to the 1st Seal… (white horse)

God showed me that heavy catastrophe must occur in order for the beast to point to the papacy (mark of the beast - Sunday worship- devil being worshipped - antichrist). There must be drama, then the papacy (antichrist), leading to "fake" peace….

the tribulation is recorded to be 7 years. The Great Tribulation is the final half, 3 1/2 years…. A time like no other……MERCY….

Matthew 24:21-24.
21 For then shall be great tribulation, such as was not since the beginning of the world to this time, no, nor ever shall be.

22 And except those days should be shortened, there should no flesh be saved: but for the elect's sake those days shall be shortened.

23 Then if any man shall say unto you, Lo, here is Christ, or there; believe it not.

24 For there shall arise false Christs, and false prophets, and shall shew great signs and wonders; insomuch that, if it were possible, they shall deceive the very elect. (KJV)

Daniel 9:27
27 And he shall confirm the covenant with many for one week: and in the midst of the week he shall cause the sacrifice and the oblation to cease, and for the overspreading of abominations he shall make it desolate, even until the consummation, and that determined shall be poured upon the desolate. (KJV)

The First Seal (Revelation 6:2)
"And I looked, and behold, a white horse! And its rider had a bow, and a crown was given to him, and he came out conquering, and to conquer."

The Second Seal (Revelation 6:4)
"And out came another horse, bright red. Its rider was permitted to take peace from the earth, so that people should slay one another, and he was given a great sword."

The Third Seal (Revelation 6:5)
"When he opened the third seal, I heard the third living creature say, "Come!" And I looked, and behold, a black horse! And its rider had a pair of scales in his hand."

The Fourth Seal (Revelation 6:7-8)
"When he opened the fourth seal, I heard the voice of the fourth living creature say, "Come!" And I looked, and behold, a pale horse! And its rider's name was Death, and Hades followed him. And they were given authority over a fourth of the earth, to kill with sword and with famine and with pestilence and by wild beasts of the earth."
Death, riding upon a pale horse, wipes out one-fourth of the earth.

The Fifth Seal (Revelation 6:9)
"When he opened the fifth seal, I saw under the altar the souls of those who had been slain for the word of God and for the witness they had borne."

Those martyred will ask God how long until He judges the earth. They are told a little while longer and given a white robe.

The Sixth Seal (Revelation 6:12-14)
"When he opened the sixth seal, I looked, and behold, there was a great earthquake, and the sun became black as sackcloth, the full moon became like blood, and the stars of the sky fell to the earth as the fig tree sheds its winter fruit when shaken by a gale. The sky vanished like a scroll that is being rolled up, and every mountain and island was removed from its place."
Catastrophic natural events take place from a rattling earthquake, the sun turning black, the moon turning blood-red, and mountains and islands disappearing.

The Seventh Seal (Revelation 8:1)
"When the Lamb opened the seventh seal, there was silence in heaven for about half an hour."
Silence fills heaven. Reminiscent of the Sabbath day of rest God took on the seventh day after creation, a brief pause occurs before the following judgments.

During these times, the deception increase. The devil wants to capture the mind. He will use all types of devices. The metaverse (funded by muons - "god particle") will be a great deception, in which the church will surrender to the papacy. End Times preaching and sharing the gospel of Christ's return, will be withheld. Sunday Law enforcement, the mark of the beast, antichrist, metaverse, etc. Heavy deception and more events will take place during this time. Violence, crime, earth's catastrophes, etc.

Last Day Events - Ellen G. White Writings
EGW Writings
Chapter 16 — The Close of Probation

When the early church became corrupted by departing from the simplicity of the gospel and accepting heathen rites and customs, she lost the Spirit and power of God; and in order to control the consciences of the people, she sought the support of the secular power. The result was the papacy, a church that controlled the power of the state, and employed it to further her own ends, especially for the punishment of "heresy." In order for the United States to form an image of the beast, the religious power must control the civil government and the authority of the state will also be employed by the church to accomplish her own ends... LDE 228.2

The "image to the beast" represents that form of apostate Protestantism which will be developed when the Protestant churches shall seek the aid of the civil power for the enforcement of their dogmas. — The Great Controversy, 443, 445 (1911). LDE 228.3

TRIBULATION HAS BEGUN

When the irrevocable decision of the sanctuary has been pronounced, and the destiny of the world has been forever fixed, the inhabitants of the earth will know it not. The forms of religion will be continued by a people from whom the Spirit of God has been finally withdrawn, and the Satanic zeal with which the prince of evil will inspire them for the accomplishment of his malignant designs will bear the semblance of zeal for God. — <u>The Great Controversy, 615 (1911)</u>.

When ministers, farmers, merchants, lawyers, great men, and professedly good men shall cry, "Peace and safety," sudden destruction cometh. Luke reports the words of Christ, that the day of God comes as a snare — the figure of an animal prowling in the woods for prey, and lo, suddenly he is entrapped in the concealed snare of the fowler. — <u>Manuscript Releases 10:266 (1876)</u>. LDE 233.1

When men are at ease, full of amusement, absorbed in buying and selling, then the thief approaches with stealthy tread. So, it will be at the coming of the Son of man. — <u>Letter 21, 1897</u>.

Red Flag:

If your congregation, is not speaking about End Times, Sharing the Gospel, and emphasizing Christ's soon return, BEWARE. **KGK**

BIBLIOGRAPHY

References (I)
[1] Fragopoulou AF, Koussoulakos SL, Margaritis LH. Cranial and postcranial skeletal variations induced in mouse embryos by mobile phone radiation. Pathophysiology. 2010;17:169-77. [PubMed][Google Scholar]
[2] Megha K, Deshmukh PS, Banerjee BD, Tripathi AK, Abegaonkar MP. Microwave radiation induced oxidative stress, cognitive impairment and inflammation in brain of Fischer rats. Indian J Exp Biol.2012;50:889-96. [PubMed] [Google Scholar]
[3] Challis LJ. Mechanisms for interaction between RF fields and biological tissue. Bioelectromagnetics.2005;(Suppl 7): S98-106. [PubMed] [Google Scholar]
[4] Leszczynski D, Joenvaara S, Reivinen J, Kuokka R. Non-thermal activation of the hsp27/p38MAPK stress pathway by mobile phone radiation in human endothelial cells: molecular mechanism for cancer- and blood-brain barrier-related effects. Differentiation. 2002;70:120-9. [PubMed] [Google Scholar]

[5] Sepehrimanesh M, Kazemipour N, Saeb M, Nazifi S. Analysis of rat testicular proteome following 30-day exposure to 900 MHz electromagnetic field radiation. Electrophoresis. 2014;35:3331-8. [PubMed][Google Scholar]

[6] Sepehrimanesh M, Kazemipour N, Saeb M, Nazifi S, Davis DL. Proteomic analysis of continuous 900-MHz radiofrequency electromagnetic field exposure in testicular tissue: a rat model of human cell phone exposure. Environ Sci Pollut Res Int. 2017;24:13666-73. [PubMed] [Google Scholar]

[7] Tkalec M, Malaric K, Pevalek-Kozlina B. Exposure to radiofrequency radiation induces oxidative stress in duckweed Lemna minor L. Sci Total Environ. 2007;388:78-89. [PubMed] [Google Scholar]

[8] Cui K, Luo X, Xu K, Ven Murthy MR. Role of oxidative stress in neurodegeneration: recent developments in assay methods for oxidative stress and nutraceutical antioxidants. Prog Neuropsychopharmacol Biol Psychiatry. 2004;28:771-99. [PubMed] [Google Scholar]

[9] Halliwell B. Role of free radicals in the neurodegenerative diseases: therapeutic implications for antioxidant treatment. Drugs Aging. 2001;18:685-716. [PubMed] [Google Scholar]

[10] Calcabrini C, Mancini U, De Bellis R, Diaz AR, Martinelli M, Cucchiarini L, et al. Effect of extremely low-frequency electromagnetic fields on antioxidant activity in the human keratinocyte cell line NCTC 2544. Biotechnol Appl Biochem. 2016 [PubMed] [Google Scholar]

[11] Venugopal SK, Devaraj S, Yang T, Jialal I. alpha-tocopherol decreases superoxide anion release in human monocytes under hyperglycemic conditions via inhibition of protein kinase C-alpha. Diabetes.2002;51:3049–54. [PubMed] [Google Scholar]
[12] Halliwell B. Oxidative stress and cancer: have we moved forward. Biochem J. 2007;401:1–11.[PubMed] [Google Scholar]
[13] Ames BN, Shigenaga MK, Hagen TM. Oxidants, antioxidants, and the degenerative diseases of aging. P Natl Acad Sci USA. 1993; 90:7915–22. [PMC free article] [PubMed] [Google Scholar]
[14] Basaga HS. Biochemical aspects of free-Radicals. Biochem Cell Biol. 1990; 68:989–98. [PubMed][Google Scholar]
[15] Stadtman ER, Oliver CN. Metal-catalyzed oxidation of proteins. J Biol Chem. 1991;256:2005.[PubMed] [Google Scholar]
[16] Feychting M, Ahlbom A. Magnetic fields and cancer in children residing near Swedish high-voltage power lines. Am J Epidemiol. 1993;138:467–81. [PubMed] [Google Scholar]
[17] Ozguner F, Altinbas A, Ozaydin M, Dogan A, Vural H, Kisioglu AN, et al. Mobile phone-induced myocardial oxidative stress: protection by a novel antioxidant agent caffeic acid phenethyl ester. Toxicol Ind Health. 2005; 21:223–30. [PubMed] [Google Scholar]
[18] Valberg PA, van Deventer TE, Repacholi MH. Workgroup report: base stations and wireless

networks-radiofrequency (RF) exposures and health consequences. Environ Health Perspect. 2007;115:416–24.[PMC free article] [PubMed] [Google Scholar]
[19] Nishiyama HIM, Kato N. Relay-by-smartphone: realizing multihop device-to-device communications. IEEE Com Mag. 2014; 52:56–65. [Google Scholar]
[20] Manikonda PK, Rajendra P, Devendranath D, Gunasekaran B, Channakeshava Aradhya RSS, et al. Influence of extremely low frequency magnetic fields on Ca2+ signaling and NMDA receptor functions in rat hippocampus. Neurosci Lett. 2007; 413:145–9. [PubMed] [Google Scholar]
[21] Soderqvist F, Carlberg M, Hardell L. Use of wireless telephones and serum S100 B levels: a descriptive cross-sectional study among healthy Swedish adults aged 18-65 years. Sci Total Environ.2009;407:798–805. [PubMed] [Google Scholar]
[22] Behari J. Biological responses of mobile phone frequency exposure. Indian J Exp Biol. 2010; 48:959–81. [PubMed] [Google Scholar]
[23] Gherardini L, Ciuti G, Tognarelli S, Cinti C. Searching for the perfect wave: the effect of radiofrequency electromagnetic fields on cells. Int J Mol Sci. 2014; 15:5366–87. [PMC free article][PubMed] [Google Scholar]
[24] Alberts B, Johnson A, Lewis J, Raff M, Roberts K, Walter P. 4th edition. New York: Garland Science; 2002. Membrane Transport of Small Molecules and

the Electrical Properties of Membranes-Molecular Biology of the Cell; p. 651. [Google Scholar]
[25] Challis LJ. Mechanisms for interaction between RF fields and biological
tissue. Bioelectromagnetics.2005: S98–106. [PubMed] [Google Scholar]
[26] Georgiou CD. Oxidative stress induced biological damage by low level EMFs: mechanism of free radical pair electron spin polarization and biochemical amplification. Eur J Oncol. 2010;5:66–113.[Google Scholar]
[27] Lobo V, Patil A, Phatak A, Chandra N. Free radicals, antioxidants and functional foods: impact on human health. Pharmacogn Rev. 2010; 4:118–26. [PMC free article] [PubMed] [Google Scholar]
[28] Chen G, Upham BL, Sun W, Chang CC, Rothwell EJ, Chen KM, et al. Effect of electromagnetic field exposure on chemically induced differentiation of friend erythroleukemia cells. Environ Health Perspect.2000;108:967–72. [PMC free article] [PubMed] [Google Scholar]
[29] Park JE, Seo YK, Yoon HH, Kim CW, Park JK, Jeon S. Electromagnetic fields induce neural differentiation of human bone marrow derived mesenchymal stem cells via ROS mediated EGFR activation. Neurochem Int. 2013; 62:418–24. [PubMed] [Google Scholar]
[30] Jajte J, Zmyslony M. [The role of melatonin in the molecular mechanism of weak, static and extremely low frequency (50 Hz) magnetic fields (ELF)] Med Pr. 2000;51:51–7. [PubMed][Google Scholar]

[31] Lai H, Singh NP. Magnetic-field-induced DNA strand breaks in brain cells of the rat. Environ Health Perspect. 2004; 112:687–94. [PMC free article] [PubMed] [Google Scholar]

[32] Aydin B, Akar A. Effects of a 900-MHz electromagnetic field on oxidative stress parameters in rat lymphoid organs, polymorphonuclear leukocytes and plasma. Arch Med Res. 2011; 42:261–7. [PubMed][Google Scholar]

[33] Dasdag S, Akdag MZ. The link between radiofrequencies emitted from wireless technologies and oxidative stress. J Chem Neuroanat. 2016;75:85–93. [PubMed] [Google Scholar]

[34] Zmyslony M, Politanski P, Rajkowska E, Szymczak W, Jajte J. Acute exposure to 930 MHz CW electromagnetic radiation in vitro affects reactive oxygen species level in rat lymphocytes treated by iron ions. Bioelectromagnetics. 2004;25:324–8. [PubMed] [Google Scholar]

[35] Wu W, Yao K, Wang KJ, Lu DQ, He JL, Xu LH, et al. Blocking 1800 MHz mobile phone radiation-induced reactive oxygen species production and DNA damage in lens epithelial cells by noise magnetic fields. Zhejiang Da Xue Bao Yi Xue Ban. 2008;37:34–8. [PubMed] [Google Scholar]

[36] Yao K, Wu W, Wang K, Ni S, Ye P, Yu Y, et al. Electromagnetic noise inhibits radiofrequency radiation-induced DNA damage and reactive oxygen species increase in human lens epithelial cells. Mol Vis. 2008;14:964–9. [PMC free article] [PubMed] [Google Scholar]

[37] Yao K, Wu W, Yu Y, Zeng Q, He J, Lu D, et al. Effect of superposed electromagnetic noise on DNA damage of lens epithelial cells induced by microwave radiation. Invest Ophthalmol Vis Sci. 2008;49:2009–15. [PubMed] [Google Scholar]

[38] Oktem F, Ozguner F, Mollaoglu H, Koyu A, Uz E. Oxidative damage in the kidney induce by 900-MHz-emitted mobile phone: protection by melatonin. Arch Med Res. 2005;36:350–5. [PubMed][Google Scholar]

[39] Friedman J, Kraus S, Hauptman Y, Schiff Y, Seger R. Mechanism of short-term ERK activation by electromagnetic fields at mobile phone frequencies. Biochem J. 2007;405:559–68. [PMC free article][PubMed] [Google Scholar]

[40] Fang YZ, Yang S, Wu G. Free radicals, antioxidants, and nutrition. Nutrition. 2002;18:872–9.[PubMed] [Google Scholar]

[41] Fridovich I. Fundamental aspects of reactive oxygen species, or what's the matterwith oxygen. Ann N Y Acad Sci. 1999;893:13–8. [PubMed] [Google Scholar]

[42] Mattson MP. Metal-catalyzed disruption of membrane protein and lipid signaling in the pathogenesis of neurodegenerative disorders. Ann N Y Acad Sci. 2004;1012:37–50. [PubMed] [Google Scholar]

[43] Halliwell B. Free radicals and antioxidants: a personal view. Nutr Rev. 1994;52:253–65. [PubMed][Google Scholar]

[44] Zmyslony M, Jajte JM. The role of free radicals in mechanisms of biological function exposed to weak, constant and net magnetic fields. Med Pr. 1998;49:177–86. [PubMed] [Google Scholar]
[45] Hoyto A, Luukkonen J, Juutilainen J, Naarala J. Proliferation, oxidative stress and cell death in cells exposed to 872 MHz radiofrequency radiation and oxidants. Radiat Res. 2008;170:235–43. [PubMed][Google Scholar]
[46] Collins T. Endothelial nuclear factor-kappa B and the initiation of the atherosclerotic lesion. Lab Invest. 1993;68:499–508. [PubMed] [Google Scholar]
[47] Lusis AJ, Navab M. Lipoprotein oxidation and gene expression in the artery wall: new opportunities for pharmacologic intervention in atherosclerosis. Biochem Pharmacol. 1993;46:2119–26. [PubMed][Google Scholar]
[48] Steinberg D, Parthasarathy S, Carew TE, Khoo JC, Witztum JL. Beyond cholesterol: modifications of low-density lipoprotein that increase its atherogenicity. N Engl J Med. 1989;320:915–24. [PubMed][Google Scholar]
[49] Oh J, Lee YD, Wagers AJ. Stem cell aging: mechanisms, regulators and therapeutic opportunities. Nat Med. 2014:870–80. [PMC free article] [PubMed] [Google Scholar]
[50] Croft RJ, Chandler JS, Burgess AP, Barry RJ, Williams JD, Clarke AR. Acute mobile phone operation affects neural function in humans. Clin Neurophysiol. 2002;113:1623–32. [PubMed] [Google Scholar]

[51] Kempson IM, Martin AL, Denman JA, French PW, Prestidge CA, Barnes TJ. Detecting the presence of denatured human serum albumin in an adsorbed protein monolayer using TOF-SIMS. Langmuir.2010;26:12075–80. [PubMed] [Google Scholar]

[52] Wu C. Heat shock transcription factors: structure and regulation. Annu Rev Cell Dev Biol.1995;11:441–69. [PubMed] [Google Scholar]

[53] Trautinger F, Kindas-Mugge I, Knobler RM, Honigsmann H. Stress proteins in the cellular response to ultraviolet radiation. J Photochem Photobiol B. 1996;35:141–8. [PubMed] [Google Scholar]

[54] Calini V, Urani C, Camatini M. Overexpression of HSP70 is induced by ionizing radiation in C3H 10T1/2 cells and protects from DNA damage. Toxicol In Vitro. 2003;17:561–6. [PubMed] [Google Scholar]

[55] Novoselova EG, Cherenkov DA, Glushkova OV, Novoselova TV, Chudnovskii VM, Iusupov VI, et al. Effect of low-intensity laser radiation (632.8 nm) on immune cells isolated from mice. Biofizika.2006;51:509–18. [PubMed] [Google Scholar]

[56] Jorge-Mora MT, Folgueiras MA, Leiro-Vidal JM, Jorge-Barreiro FJ, Ares-Pena FJ, Lopez-Martin E. Exposure to 2.45 GHz microwave radiation provokes cerebral changes in induction of HSP90 heat shock protein in rat. Prog Electromagn Res. 2010;100:351–79. [Google Scholar]

[57] George I, Geddis MS, Lill Z, Lin H, Gomez T, Blank M, et al. Myocardial function improved by electromagnetic field induction of stress protein hsp 70. J Cell Physiol. 2008;216:816-23. [PMC free article] [PubMed] [Google Scholar]
[58] Shi B, Farboud B, Nuccitelli R, Isseroff RR. Power-line frequency electromagnetic fields do not induce changes in phosphorylation, localization or expression of the 27-kiloDalton heat shock protein in human keratinocytes. Environ Health Perspect. 2003;111:281-8. [PMC free article] [PubMed][Google Scholar]
[59] Ramaglia V, Buck LT. Time-dependent expression of heat shock proteins 70 and 90 in tissues of the anoxic western painted turtle. J Exp Biol. 2004;207:3775-84. [PubMed] [Google Scholar]
[60] Yang J. Frequency shifts in a piezoelectric body due to small amounts of additional mass on its surface. IEEE Trans Ultrason Ferroelectr Freq Control. 2004;51:1199-202. [PubMed] [Google Scholar]
[61] Grigor'ev IuG. The electromagnetic fields of cellular phones and the health of children and of teenagers (the situation requiring to take an urgent measure) Radiats Biol Radioecol. 2005;45:442-50.[PubMed] [Google Scholar]
[62] Oscar KJ, Hawkins TD. Microwave alteration of the blood-brain barrier system of rats. Brain Res.1977;126:281-93. [PubMed] [Google Scholar]
[63] Nittby H, Grafstrom G, Eberhardt JL, Malmgren L, Brun A, Persson BR, et al. Radiofrequency and

extremely low-frequency electromagnetic field effects on the blood-brain barrier. Electromagn Biol Med.2008;27:103–26. [PubMed] [Google Scholar]
[64] Castelnau PA, Garrett RS, Palinski W, Witztum JL, Campbell IL, Powell HC. Abnormal iron deposition associated with lipid peroxidation in transgenic mice expressing interleukin-6 in the brain. J Neuropathol Exp Neurol. 1998;57:268–82. [PubMed] [Google Scholar]
[65] Thompson KJ, Shoham S, Connor JR. Iron and neurodegenerative disorders. Brain Res Bull.2001;55:155–64. [PubMed] [Google Scholar]
[66] Herbert MR, Sage C. Autism and EMF. Plausibility of a pathophysiological link--Part I?Pathophysiology. 2013;20:191–209. [PubMed] [Google Scholar]
[67] Thomas RH, Meeking MM, Mepham JR, Tichenoff L, Possmayer F, Liu S, et al. The enteric bacterial metabolite propionic acid alters brain and plasma phospholipid molecular species: further development of a rodent model of autism spectrum disorders. J Neuroinflammation. 2012;9:153. [PMC free article][PubMed] [Google Scholar]
[68] Onore CE, Nordahl CW, Young GS, Van de Water JA, Rogers SJ, Ashwood P. Levels of soluble platelet endothelial cell adhesion molecule-1 and P-selectin are decreased in children with autism spectrum disorder. Biol Psychiatry. 2012;72:1020–5. [PMC free article] [PubMed] [Google Scholar]
[69] Ozmen I, Naziroglu M, Alici HA, Sahin F, Cengiz M, Eren I. Spinal morphine administration

reduces the fatty acid contents in spinal cord and brain by increasing oxidative stress. Neurochem Res. 2007;32:19–25. [PubMed] [Google Scholar]
[70] Deshmukh PS, Megha K, Banerjee BD, Ahmed RS, Chandna S, Abegaonkar MP, et al. Detection of low level microwave radiation induced deoxyribonucleic acid damage vis-a-vis genotoxicity in brain of fischer rats. Toxicol Int. 2013;20:19–24. [PMC free article] [PubMed] [Google Scholar]
[71] Odaci E, Bas O, Kaplan S. Effects of prenatal exposure to a 900 MHz electromagnetic field on the dentate gyrus of rats: a stereological and histopathological study. Brain Res. 2008;1238:224–9. [PubMed][Google Scholar]
[72] Erdem Koc, Kaplan S, Altun G, Gumus H, Gulsum Deniz O, Aydin I, et al. Neuroprotective effects of melatonin and omega-3 on hippocampal cells prenatally exposed to 900 MHz electromagnetic fields. Int J Radiat Biol. 2016;92:590–5. [PubMed] [Google Scholar]
[73] Volkow ND, Tomasi D, Wang GJ, Vaska P, Fowler JS, Telang F, et al. Effects of cell phone radiofrequency signal exposure on brain glucose metabolism. JAMA. 2011;305:808–13. [PMC free article][PubMed] [Google Scholar]
[74] Tasset I, Medina FJ, Jimena I, Aguera E, Gascon F, Feijoo M, et al. Neuroprotective effects of extremely low-frequency electromagnetic fields on a Huntington's disease rat model: effects on neurotrophic factors and neuronal

density. Neuroscience. 2012;209:54–63. [PubMed] [Google Scholar]

[75] Kivrak EG. Samsun, Turkey: Ondokuz Mayis University; 2014. Investigation of the effects of boswellia sacra and folic acid on hippocampus with electromagnetic fields Master thesis. [Google Scholar]

[76] Johansen C. Electromagnetic fields and health effects-epidemiologic studies of cancer, diseases of the central nervous system and arrhythmia-related heart disease. Scand J Work Environ Health. 2004;30(Suppl 1):1–30. [PubMed] [Google Scholar]

[77] Rubin GJ, Hahn G, Everitt BS, Cleare AJ, Wessely S. Are some people sensitive to mobile phone signals: within participants double blind randomised provocation study. BMJ. 2006;332:886–91.[PMC free article] [PubMed] [Google Scholar]

[78] Haynal A, Regli F. Amyotrophic lateral sclerosis associated with accumulated electric injury. Confin Neurol. 1964;24:189–98. [PubMed] [Google Scholar]

[79] Maskey D, Kim M, Aryal B, Pradhan J, Choi IY, Park KS, et al. Effect of 835 MHz radiofrequency radiation exposure on calcium binding proteins in the hippocampus of the mouse brain. Brain Res.2010;1313:232–41. [PubMed] [Google Scholar]

[80] Villeneuve PJ, Agnew DA, Johnson KC, Mao Y. Canadian Cancer Registries Epidemiology Research G. Brain cancer and occupational exposure to magnetic fields among men: results from a Canadian population-based case-control study. Int J Epidemiol. 2002;31:210–7. [PubMed] [Google Scholar]

[81] Othman SB, Yabe T. Use of hydrogen peroxide and peroxyl radicals to induce oxidative stress in neuronal cells. Reviews in Agricultural Science. 2015;3:40-5. [Google Scholar]
[82] Kesari KK, Kumar S, Behari J. 900-MHz microwave radiation promotes oxidation in rat brain.Electromagn Biol Med. 2011;30:219-34. [PubMed] [Google Scholar]
[83] Atli Sekeroglu Z, Akar A, Sekeroglu V. Evaluation of the cytogenotoxic damage in immature and mature rats exposed to 900 MHz radiofrequency electromagnetic fields. Int J Radiat Biol. 2013;89:985-92.[PubMed] [Google Scholar]
[84] Liu C, Gao P, Xu SC, Wang Y, Chen CH, He MD, et al. Mobile phone radiation induces mode-dependent DNA damage in a mouse spermatocyte-derived cell line: a protective role of melatonin. Int J Radiat Biol. 2013;89:993-1001. [PubMed] [Google Scholar]
[85] Ruediger HW. Genotoxic effects of radiofrequency electromagnetic fields. Pathophysiology.2009;16:89-102. [PubMed] [Google Scholar]
[86] Kryston TB, Georgiev AB, Pissis P, Georgakilas AG. Role of oxidative stress and DNA damage in human carcinogenesis. Mutat Res. 2011;711:193-201. [PubMed] [Google Scholar]
[87] Henderson PT, Evans MD, Cooke MS. Salvage of oxidized guanine derivatives in the (2'-deoxy) ribonucleotide pool as source of mutations in

DNA. Mutat Res. 2010;703:11-7. [PMC free article][PubMed] [Google Scholar]
[88] Tothova L, Kamodyova N, Cervenka T, Celec P. Salivary markers of oxidative stress in oral diseases.Front Cell Infect Microbiol. 2015;5:73. [PMC free article] [PubMed] [Google Scholar]
[89] Aitken RJ, Harkiss D, Buckingham DW. Analysis of lipid peroxidation mechanisms in human spermatozoa. Mol Reprod Dev. 1993;35:302-15. [PubMed] [Google Scholar]
[90] Agarwal A, Saleh RA. Role of oxidants in male infertility: rationale, significance, and treatment. Urol Clin North Am. 2002;29:817-27. [PubMed] [Google Scholar]
[91] Nelson JF, Karelus K, Bergman MD, Felicio LS. Neuroendocrine involvement in aging: evidence from studies of reproductive aging and caloric restriction. Neurobiol Aging. 1995;16:837-43. discussion 55-6. [PubMed] [Google Scholar]
[92] Erogul O, Oztas E, Yildirim I, Kir T, Aydur E, Komesli G, et al. Effects of electromagnetic radiation from a cellular phone on human sperm motility: an in vitro study. Arch Med Res. 2006;37:840-3.[PubMed] [Google Scholar]
[93] Goldhaber MK, Polen MR, Hiatt RA. The risk of miscarriage and birth defects among women who use visual display terminals during pregnancy. Am J Ind Med. 1988;13:695-706. [PubMed][Google Scholar]
[94] Forgacs Z, Somosy Z, Kubinyi G, Bakos J, Hudak A, Surjan A, et al. Effect of whole-body 1800 MHz GSM-like microwave exposure on testicular

steroidogenesis and histology in mice. Reprod Toxicol.2006;22:111–7. [PubMed] [Google Scholar]
[95] Ozguner M, Koyu A, Cesur G, Ural M, Ozguner F, Gokcimen A, et al. Biological and morphological effects on the reproductive organ of rats after exposure to electromagnetic field. Saudi Med J.2005;26:405–10. [PubMed] [Google Scholar]
[96] Ghodbane SLA, Ammari M, Sakly M, Abdelmelek H. Does static magnetic field-exposure induced oxidative stress and apoptosis in rat kidney and muscle. Effect of vitamin E and selenium supplementations? Gen Physiol Biophys. 2015;34:23–32. [PubMed] [Google Scholar]
[97] Meral I, Mert H, Mert N, Deger Y, Yoruk I, Yetkin A, et al. Effects of 900-MHz electromagnetic field emitted from cellular phone on brain oxidative stress and some vitamin levels of guinea pigs. Brain Res.2007;1169:120–4. [PubMed] [Google Scholar]
[98] Misa-Agustino MJ, Leiro-Vidal JM, Gomez-Amoza JL, Jorge-Mora MT, Jorge-Barreiro FJ, Salas-Sanchez AA, et al. EMF radiation at 2450 MHz triggers changes in the morphology and expression of heat shock proteins and glucocorticoid receptors in rat thymus. Life Sci. 2015;127:1–11. [PubMed][Google Scholar]
[99] Balci M, Devrim E, Durak I. Effects of mobile phones on oxidant/antioxidant balance in cornea and lens of rats. Curr Eye Res. 2007;32:21–5. [PubMed] [Google Scholar]
[100] Bodera P, Stankiewicz W, Zawada K, Antkowiak B, Paluch M, Kieliszek J, et al. Changes in

antioxidant capacity of blood due to mutual action of electromagnetic field (1800 MHz) and opioid drug (tramadol) in animal model of persistent inflammatory state. Pharmacol Rep. 2013;65:421–8. [PubMed][Google Scholar]

[101] Ozorak A, Naziroglu M, Celik O, Yuksel M, Ozcelik D, Ozkaya MO, et al. Wi-Fi (2.45 GHz)- and mobile phone (900 and 1800 MHz)-Induced risks on oxidative stress and elements in kidney and testis of rats during pregnancy and the development of offspring. biol trace elem Res. 2013;156:221–9. [PubMed][Google Scholar]

[102] Ozgur E, Guler G, Seyhan N. Mobile phone radiation-induced free radical damage in the liver is inhibited by the antioxidants N-acetyl cysteine and epigallocatechin-gallate. Int J Radiat Biol.2010;86:935–45. [PubMed] [Google Scholar]

[103] Ikinci A, Mercantepe T, Unal D, Erol HS, Sahin A, Aslan A, et al. Morphological and antioxidant impairments in the spinal cord of male offspring rats following exposure to a continuous 900 MHz electromagnetic field during early and mid-adolescence. J Chem Neuroanat. 2016;75:99–104. [PubMed][Google Scholar]

[104] Gurler HS, Bilgici B, Akar AK, Tomak L, Bedir A. Increased DNA oxidation (8-OHdG) and protein oxidation (AOPP) by low level electromagnetic field (2.45 GHz) in rat brain and protective effect of garlic.Int J Radiat. Biol. 2014;90:892–6. [PubMed] [Google Scholar]

[105] Turedi S, Kerimoglu G, Mercantepe T, Odaci E. Biochemical and pathological changes in the male rat kidney and bladder following exposure to continuous 900-MHz electromagnetic field on postnatal days 22-59. Int J Radiat Biol. 2017:1-10. [PubMed] [Google Scholar]

[106] Yan JG, Agresti M, Bruce T, Yan YH, Granlund A, Matloub HS. Effects of cellular phone emissions on sperm motility in rats. Fertil Steril. 2007;88:957-64. [PubMed] [Google Scholar]

[107] Rajkovic V, Matavulj M, Gledic D, Lazetic B. Evaluation of rat thyroid gland morphophysiological status after three months exposure to 50 Hz electromagnetic field. Tissue Cell. 2003;35:223-31. [PubMed] [Google Scholar]

[108] Deniz OG, Kivrak EG, Kaplan AA, Altunkaynak BZ. Effects of folic acid on rat kidney exposed to 900 MHz electromagnetic radiation. JMAU. 2017:900. in press. [Google Scholar]

[109] Wang XW, Ding GR, Shi CH, Zhao T, Zhang J, Zeng LH, et al. Effect of electromagnetic pulse exposure on permeability of blood-testicle barrier in mice. Biomed Environ Sci. 2008;21:218-21.[PubMed] [Google Scholar]

[110] Avendano C, Mata A, Sarmiento CAS, Doncel GF. Use of laptop computers connected to internet through Wi-Fi decreases human sperm motility and increases sperm DNA fragmentation. Fertil Steril.2012;97:39–U93. [PubMed] [Google Scholar]

[111] Narayanan SN, Kumar RS, Kedage V, Nalini K, Nayak S, Bhat PG. Evaluation ol oxidant stress and

antioxidant defense in discrete brain regions of rats exposed to 900 MHz radiation. Bratisl Med J.2014;115:260–6. [Google Scholar]

[112] Hanci H, Türedi S, Topal Z, Mercantepe T, Bozkurt I, Kaya H, et al. Can prenatal exposure to a 900 MHz electromagnetic field affect the morphology of the spleen and thymus, and alter biomarkers of oxidative damage in 21-day-old male rats? Biotech Histochem. 2015;90:535–43. [PubMed][Google Scholar]

[113] Lantow M, Lupke M, Frahm J, Mattsson MO, Kuster N, Simko M. ROS release and Hsp70 expression after exposure to 1,800 MHz radiofrequency electromagnetic fields in primary human monocytes and lymphocytes. Radiat Environ Biophys. 2006;45:55–62. [PubMed] [Google Scholar]

[114] Baohong W, Lifen J, Lanjuan L, Jianlin L, Deqiang L, Wei Z, et al. Evaluating the combinative effects on human lymphocyte DNA damage induced by ultraviolet ray C plus 1.8 GHz microwaves using comet assay in vitro . Toxicology. 2007;232:311–6. [PubMed] [Google Scholar]

[115] Ansarihadipour H, Bayatiani M. Influence of electromagnetic fields on lead toxicity: a study of conformational changes in human blood proteins. Iran Red Crescent Med J. 2016;18:e28050.[PMC free article] [PubMed] [Google Scholar]

[116] Belyaev IY, Hillert L, Protopopova M, Tamm C, Malmgren LO, Persson BR, et al. 915 MHz microwaves and 50 Hz magnetic field affect

chromatin conformation and 53BP1 foci in human lymphocytes from hypersensitive and healthy persons. Bioelectromagnetics. 2005;26:173–84. [PubMed][Google Scholar]

[117] Agarwal A, Desai NR, Makker K, Varghese A, Mouradi R, Sabanegh E, et al. Effects of radiofrequency electromagnetic waves (RF-EMW) from cellular phones on human ejaculated semen: an in vitro pilot study. Fertil Steril. 2009;92:1318–25. [PubMed] [Google Scholar]

[118] Lewicka M, Henrykowska GA, Pacholski K, Smigielski J, Rutkowski M, Dziedziczak-Buczynska M, et al. The effect of electromagnetic radiation emitted by display screens on cell oxygen metabolism – in vitro studies. Arch Med Sci. 2015;11:1330–9. [PMC free article] [PubMed] [Google Scholar]

[119] Lu YS, Huang BT, Huang YX. Reactive oxygen species formation and apoptosis in human peripheral blood mononuclear cell induced by 900 MHz mobile phone radiation. Oxid Med Cell Longev.2012;2012:740280. [PMC free article] [PubMed] [Google Scholar]

[120] De Iuliis GN, Newey RJ, King BV, Aitken RJ. Mobile phone radiation induces reactive oxygen species production and DNA damage in human spermatozoa in vitro . PLoS One. 2009;4:e6446.[PMC free article] [PubMed] [Google Scholar]

[121] Sefidbakht Y, Moosavi-Movahedi AA, Hosseinkhani S, Khodagholi F, Torkzadeh-Mahani M, Foolad F, et al. Effects of 940 MHz EMF on

bioluminescence and oxidative response of stable luciferase producing HEK cells. Photochem Photobiol Sci. 2014;13:1082–92. [PubMed] [Google Scholar]
[122] Goraca A, Ciejka E, Piechota A. Effects of extremely low frequency magnetic field on the parameters of oxidative stress in heart. J Physiol Pharmacol. 2010;61:333–8. [PubMed] [Google Scholar]
[123] Halliwell B. How to characterize an antioxidant- an update. Biochem Soc Symp. 1995;61:73–101.[PubMed] [Google Scholar]
[124] Rice-Evans CA, Diplock AT. Current status of antioxidant therapy. Free Radic Biol Med.1993;15:77–96. [PubMed] [Google Scholar]
[125] Krinsky NI. Mechanism of action of biological antioxidants. Proc Soc Exp Biol Med. 1992;200:248–54. [PubMed] [Google Scholar]
[126] Di Loreto S, Falone S, Caracciolo V, Sebastiani P, D'Alessandro A, Mirabilio A, et al. Fifty hertz extremely low-frequency magnetic field exposure elicits redox and trophic response in rat-cortical neurons.J Cell Physiol. 2009;219:334–43. [PubMed] [Google Scholar]
[127] Sun W, Gan Y, Fu Y, Lu D, Chiang H. An incoherent magnetic field inhibited EGF receptor clustering and phosphorylation induced by a 50-Hz magnetic field in cultured FL cells. Cell Physiol Biochem. 2008;22:507–14. [PubMed] [Google Scholar]
[128] E.N. Antioxidant defenses in eukaryotic cells. Basel, Switzerland: Birkhauser Verlag; 1993.[Google Scholar]

[129] Zhao X, Alexander JS, Zhang S, Zhu Y, Sieber NJ, Aw TY, et al. Redox regulation of endothelial barrier integrity. Am J Physiol Lung Cell Mol Physiol. 2001;281:L879–86. [PubMed] [Google Scholar]

[130] Aslan L, Meral I. Effect of oral vitamin E supplementation on oxidative stress in guinea-pigs with short-term hypothermia. Cell Biochem Funct. 2007;25:711–5. [PubMed] [Google Scholar]

[131] Awad SM, Hassan NS. Health Risks of electromagnetic radiation from mobile phone on brain of rats.Journal of Applied Sciences Research. 2008;4:1994–2000. [Google Scholar]

[132] Luo X, Chen M, Duan Y, Duan W, Zhang H, He Y, et al. Chemoprotective action of lotus seedpod procyanidins on oxidative stress in mice induced by extremely low-frequency electromagnetic field exposure. Biomed Pharmacother. 2016;82:640–8. [PubMed] [Google Scholar]

[133] Singh HP, Sharma VP, Batish DR, Kohli RK. Cell phone electromagnetic field radiations affect rhizogenesis through impairment of biochemical processes. Environ Monit Assess. 2012;184:1813–21.[PubMed] [Google Scholar]

[134] Sepehrimanesh M, Nazifi S, Saeb M, Kazemipour N. Effect of 900 MHz radiofrequency electromagnetic field exposure on serum and testicular tissue antioxidantenzymes of rat. Online Journal of Veterinary Research. 2016;20(9):617–24. [Google Scholar]

[135] Tkalec M, Stambuk A, Srut M, Malaric K, Klobucar GI. Oxidative and genotoxic effects of 900 MHz electromagnetic fields in the earthworm Eisenia fetida. Ecotoxicol Environ Saf. 2013;90:7–12.[PubMed] [Google Scholar]
[136] Lanir A, Schejter A. On the sixth coordination position of beef liver catalase. Febs Lett.1975;55:254–6. [PubMed] [Google Scholar]
[137] Ozturk A, Baltaci AK, Mogulkoc R, Oztekin E. Zinc prevention of electromagnetically induced damage to rat testicle and kidney tissues. Biol Trace Elem Res. 2003;96:247–54. [PubMed][Google Scholar]
[138] Martinez-Samano JTP, Rez-Oropeza MA, Elias-Vinas D, Verdugo-Díaz L. Effects of acute electromagnetic field exposure and movement restraint on antioxidant system in liver, heart, kidney and plasma of Wistar rats: a preliminary report. Int J Radiat Biol. 2010;86:1088–94. [PubMed][Google Scholar]
[139] Devrim E, Ergüder I, Kiliçoglu B, Yaykasli E, Cetin R, Durak I. Effects of electromagnetic radiation use on oxidant/antioxidant status and DNA turn-over enzyme activities in erythrocytes and heart, kidney, liver, and ovary tissues from rats: possible protective role of vitamin C. Toxicol Mech Methods.2008;18:679 6–83. [PubMed] [Google Scholar]
[140] Odaci E, Unal D, Mercantepe T, Topal Z, Hanci H, Turedi S, et al. Pathological effects of prenatal exposure to a 900 MHz electromagnetic field on the 21-day-old male rat kidney. Biotech

Histochem.2015;90:93–101. [PubMed] [Google Scholar]
[141] Kinnula VL, Paakko P, Soini Y. Antioxidant enzymes and redox regulating thiol proteins in malignancies of human lung. FEBS Lett. 2004;569:1–6. [PubMed] [Google Scholar]
[142] Sokolovic D, Djindjic B, Nikolic J, Bjelakovic G, Pavlovic D, Kocic G, et al. Melatonin reduces oxidative stress induced by chronic exposure of microwave radiation from mobile phones in rat brain. J Radiat Res. 2008;49:579–86. [PubMed] [Google Scholar]
[143] Ozguner F, Oktem F, Ayata A, Koyu A, Yilmaz HR. A novel antioxidant agent caffeic acid phenethyl ester prevents long-term mobile phone exposure-induced renal impairment in rat Prognostic value of malondialdehyde. N-acetyl-beta-D-glucosaminidase and nitric oxide determination. Mol Cell Biochem.2005;277:73–80. [PubMed] [Google Scholar]
[144] Fang YZ, Yang S, Wu GY. Free radicals, antioxidants, and nutrition. Nutrition. 2002;18:872–9.[PubMed] [Google Scholar]
[145] Martinez-Samano J, Torres-Duran PV, Juarez-Oropeza MA, Verdugo-Diaz L. Effect of acute extremely low frequency electromagnetic field exposure on the antioxidant status and lipid levels in rat brain. Arch Med Res. 2012;43:183–9. [PubMed] [Google Scholar]
[146] Ghanbari AA, Shabani K, Mohammad nejad D. protective effects of vitamin e consumption against 3MT electromagnetic field effects on oxidative

parameters in substantia nigra in rats. Basic Clin Neurosci.2016;7:315–22. [PMC free article] [PubMed] [Google Scholar]
[147] de Moffarts B, Kirschvink N, Art T, Pincemail J, Lekeux P. Effect of oral antioxidant supplementation on blood antioxidant status in trained thoroughbred horses. Vet J. 2005;169:65–74.[PubMed] [Google Scholar]
[148] Ulubay M, Yahyazadeh A, Deniz OG, Kivrak EG, Altunkaynak BZ, Erdem G, et al. Effects of prenatal 900 MHz electromagnetic field exposures on the histology of rat kidney. Int J Radiat Biol.2015;91:35–41. [PubMed] [Google Scholar]
[149] Ralston NVC, Ralston CR, Blackwell JL, Raymond LJ. Dietary and tissue selenium in relation to methylmercury toxicity. Neurotoxicology. 2008;29:802–11. [PubMed] [Google Scholar]
[150] Zhang J, Zhang YH, Jiang RP, Lian ZS, Wang H, Luo R, et al. Protective effects of vitamin E against electromagnetic radiation from cell phones in pregnant and fetal rats' brain tissues. Journal of Shandong University (Health Sciences) 2011;9:9–14. [Google Scholar]
[151] Oral B, Guney M, Ozguner F, Karahan N, Mungan T, Comlekci S, et al. Endometrial apoptosis induced by a 900-MHz mobile phone: preventive effects of vitamins E and C. Adv Ther. 2006;23:957–73.[PubMed] [Google Scholar]
[152] Mohammadnejad D, Rad JS, Azami A, Lotfi A. Role of vitamin E in prevention of damages in the

thymus induced by electromagnetic field: ultrastructural and light microscopic studies. Bulletin of the Veterinary Institute in Pulawy. 2011;55:111–5. [Google Scholar]
[153] Traber MG. Vitamin E regulatory mechanisms. Annu Rev Nutr. 2007;27:347–62. [PubMed][Google Scholar]
[154] Wang X, Fenech M. A comparison of folic acid and 5-methyltetrahydrofolate for prevention of DNA damage and cell death in human lymphocytes in vitro . Mutagenesis. 2003;18:81–6. [PubMed][Google Scholar]
[155] Hardeland R, Pandi-Perumal SR, Cardinali DP. Melatonin. Int J Biochem Cell Biol. 2006;38:313–6.[PubMed] [Google Scholar]
[156] Hardeland R. Antioxidative protection by melatonin: multiplicity ofmechanisms from radical detoxification to radical avoidance. Endocrine. 2005;27:119–30. [PubMed] [Google Scholar]
[157] Tan DX, Poeggeler B, Manchester LC, Reiter RJ. Melatonin: a potent, endogenous hydroxyl radical scavenger. Endocrine J. 1993;1:57–60. [Google Scholar]
[158] DAWN Lowes, Murphy MP, Galley HF. Antioxidants that protect mitochondria reduce interleukin-6 and oxidative stress, improve mitochondrial function, and reduce biochemical markers of organ dysfunction in a rat model of acute sepsis. Anaesth. 2013;110:472–80. [PMC free article] [PubMed][Google Scholar]

[159] Reiter RJ, Herman TS, Meltz ML. Melatonin and radioprotection from genetic damage: in vivo/in vitro studies with human volunteers. Mutat Res. 1996;371:221-8. [PubMed] [Google Scholar]
[160] Reiter RJ, Herman TS, Meltz ML. Melatonin reduces gamma radiation-induced primary DNA damage in human blood lymphocytes. Mutat Res. 1998;397:203-8. [PubMed] [Google Scholar]
[161] Shirazi A, Ghobadi G, Ghazi-Khansari M. A radiobiological review onmelatonin: a novel radioprotector. J Radiat Res. 2007;48:263-72. [PubMed] [Google Scholar]
[162] Ozguner F, Aydin G, Mollaoglu H, Gokalp O, Koyu A, Cesur G. Prevention of mobile phone induced skin tissue changes by melatonin in rat: an experimental study. Toxicol Ind Health. 2004;20:133-9.[PubMed] [Google Scholar]

Articles from Journal of Microscopy and Ultrastructure are provided here courtesy of Wolters Kluwer -- Medknow Publications

References (II)
1. Michaelson, S. M. 1986. Interaction of unmodulated radiofrequency fields with living matter: Experimental results. Pp. 339-423 in Handbook of Biological Effects of Electromagnetic Fields, C. Polk, editor, and E. Postow, editor. , eds. Boca Raton, FL.

2. McRee, D. I., and H. Wachtel. 1980. The effects of microwave radiation on the vitality of isolated frog sciatic nerves. Radiat. Res. 82:536-546. [PubMed]McRee, D. I., and H. Wachtel. 1982. Pulse microwave effects on nerve vitality. Radiat. Res. 91:212-218. [PubMed]

4. Wachtel, H., R. Seaman, and W. Joines. 1975. Effects of low-intensity microwaves on isolated neurons. Ann. NY Acad. Sci. 247:46-62. [PubMed]

5. Chou, C.-K.and A. W. Guy. 1973. Effect of 2450 MHz microwave fields on peripheral nerves. Pp. 318-310 in Digest of Technical Papers. IEEE International Microwave Symposium (Boulder, CO, June 1973).

6. Courtney, K. R., J. C. Lin, A. W. Guy, and C.-K. Chou. 1975. Microwave effect on rabbit superior cervical ganglion. IEEE Trans. Microwave Theory Tech. MTT-23: 809-813.

7. Liddle, C. G., and C. F. Blackman. 1984. Endocrine, physiological and biochemical effects. Pp. 5.79-5.93 in Biological Effects of Radiofrequency Radiation, J. A. Elder, editor, and D. F. Cahill, editor. , eds. U.S.E.P.A. Report No. EPA-600/8-83-026F. Research Triangle Park, NC: Health Effects Research Laboratory, United States Environmental Protection Agency8. Chapman, R. M., and C. A. Cain. 1975. Absence of heart rate effects in isolated frog heart with pulse modulated microwave energy. J. Microwave Power 13:411-419. [PubMed]

9. Yee, K.-C., C.-K. Chou, and A. W. Guy. 1984. Effect of microwave radiation on the beating rate of isolated frog hearts. Bioelectromagnetics 5:263-270. [PubMed]

10.
Yee, K.-C., C.-K. Chou, A. W. Guy. 1988. Influence of microwaves on the beating rate of isolated rat hearts. Bioelectromagnetics 9: 175-181. [PubMed]

11.
World Health Organization Environmental Health Criteria. 1991. Electromagnetic Fields (300 Hz-300 GHz). Geneva, Switzerland: WHO

12. Schwartz, J.-L., D. E. House, and G. A. R. Mealing. 1990. Exposure of frog hearts to CW or amplitude-modulated VHF fields: Selective efflux of calcium ions at 16 Hz. Bioelectromagnetics 11:349-358. [PubMed

13. Johnson, C. C., and A. W. Guy. 1972. Nonionizing electromagnetic wave effects in biological materials and systems. Proc. IEEE 60:692-718.

14.Servantie, A.M., and J. Etienne.
1975. Synchronization of cortical neurons by a pulsed microwave field as evidenced by spectral analysis of electrocorticograms from the white rat. Ann. NY Acad. Sci. 247:82-86. [PubMed]

15. Lai, H., M. A. Carino, A. Horita, and A. W. Guy. 1989. Low-level microwave irradiation and central cholinergic activity: A dose-response
study. Bioelectromagnetics 10:203-208. [PubMed]

16 Bawin, S. M., R. J. Gavalas-Medici, W. R. Adey. 1973. Effects of modulated very high frequency fields on specific brain rhythms in cats. Brain Res. 58:365-384. [PubMed]

17.dey, W. R., S. M. Bawin, and A. F. Lawrence. 1982. Effects of weak amplitude-modulated

microwave fields on calcium efflux from awake cat cerebral cortex. Bioelectromagnetics 3:295-307. [PubMed]
18. Merritt, J. H., W. W. Shelton, and A. F. Chamness. 1982. Attempts to alter 45Ca2+ binding to brain tissue with pulse-modulated microwave energy. Bioelectromagnetics 3:475-478. [PubMed]
19. Michaelson, S. M., and J. C. Lin. 1987. Biological Effects and Health Implications of Radiofrequency Radiation. New York, NY: Plenum Press.
20. Justesen, D. R. 1980. Microwave irradiation and the blood-brain barrier. Proc. IEEE 68:60-67.
21. Williams, W. M., S. T. Lu, M. Del Cerro, and S. M. Michaelson. 1984. Effect of 2450 MHz microwave energy on the blood-brain barrier to hydrophilic tracers. Brain Res. Rev. 7:191-212. [PubMed]
22. Anderson, L. E., and R. D. Phillips. 1985. Biological effects of electric fields: An overview. Pp. 345-378 in Biological Effects and Dosimetry of Static and ELF Electromagnetic Fields, M. Grandolfo, editor, S. M. Michaelson, editor, and A. Rindi, editor. , eds. New York, NY: Plenum Press.
23. enforde, T. S., and T. F. Budinger. 1986. Biological effects and physical safety aspects of NMR imaging and in vivo spectroscopy. Pp. 493-548 in NMR in Medicine: Instrumentation and Clinical Applications, S. R. Thomas, editor, and R. L. Dixon, editor. , eds. Medical Physics Monograph No. 14. New York, NY: American Association of Physicists in Medicine.
24. Wachtel, H. 1978. Firing-pattern changes and transmembrane currents are produced by extremely

low frequency fields in pacemaker neurons. Pp. 132-146 in Biological Effects of Extremely Low Frequency Electromagnetic Fields, R. D. Phillips, editor, M. F. Gillis, editor, W. T. Kaune, editor, and D. D. Mahlum, editor. , eds. U.S. Department of Energy Technical Information Center Report No. CONF-781016. Springfield, VA: National Technical Information Service.
25.
Graham, C., M. R. Cook, and H. D. Cohen. 1990. Immunological and Biochemical Effects of 60-Hz Electric and Magnetic Fields in Humans. Midwest Research Institute Final Report for Contract No. DE-FCO1-84-CE76246 (Order No. DE90006671). Oak Ridge, TN: U.S. Department of Energy, Office of Scientific and Technical Information.
26.
Carpenter, R. L., and C. A. Van Ummerson. 1968. The action of microwave power on the eye. J. Microwave Power 3:3-19.
Guy, A. W., J. C. Lin, P. O. Kramar, and A. F. Emery. 1975. Effect of 2450 MHz radiation on the rabbit eye.IEEE Trans. Microwave Theory Tech. MTT-23:492-498.
28. Kramar, P., C. Harris, A. F. Emery, A. W. Guy. 1978. Acute microwave irradiation and cataract formation in rabbits and monkeys. J. Microwave Power 13:239-249. [PubMed]
9. Monohan, J. C., H. A. Kues, D. S. McLeod, S. A. D'Anna, and G A. Lutty. 1988. Lowering of microwave exposure threshold for induction of

primate ocular effects by timolol maleate. Bioelectromagnetics Society Tenth Annual Meeting, Abstract B-07-1, p. 48 (Stamford, CT, June 1988).

30. enforde, T. S. 1990. Biological effects of extremely low frequency magnetic fields. Pp. 291-315 in Extremely Low Frequency Electromagnetic Fields: The Question of Cancer, B. W. Wilson, editor, R. G. Stevens, editor, and L. E. Anderson, editor. , eds. Columbus, OH: Battelle Press.

31.Lovsund, P., P. A. Oberg, S. E. G. Nilsson, and T. Reuter. 1980. Magnetophosphenes: A quantitative analysis of thresholds. Med. Biol. Eng. Comput. 18:326-334. [PubMed]

32.Lovsund, P., P. A. Oberg, and S. E. G. Nilsson. 1980. Magneto-and electrophosphenes: A comparative study.Med. Biol. Eng. Comput. 18: 758-764. [PubMed]

33.Silny, J. 1986. The influence threshold of a time-varying magnetic field in the human organism. Pp. 105-112 in Biological Effects of Static and Extremely Low Frequency Magnetic Fields, J. H. Bernhardt, editor. , ed. Munich, Germany: MMV Medizin Verlag.

34.Lotz, W. G., S. M. Michaelson. 1978. Temperature and corticosterone relationships in microwave-exposed rats.J. Appl. Physiol. Resp. Envir. Exercise Physiol. 47:438-445. [PubMed]

35.Lotz, W. G., and S. M. Michaelson. 1979. Effects of hypophysectomy and dexamethasone on rat adrenal response to microwaves. J. Appl. Physiol. Resp. Envir. Exercise Physiol. 47:1284-1288. [PubMed]

6.Lu, S.-T., W. G. Lotz, and S. M. Michaelson. 1980. a. Advances in microwave-induced neuroendocrine effects: The concept of stress. Proc. IEEE 68:73-1. [PubMed]

40. Lymangrover, J. R., E. Kekn, and Y. J. Seto. 1983. 60-Hz electric field alters the steroidogenic response of rat adrenal tissue in vitro. Life Sci. 32:691-696. [PubMed]

41. Wolpaw, J. R., R. F. Seegal, R. I. Dowman, and S. Satya-Murti. 1987. Chronic Effects of 60-Hz Electric and Magnetic Fields on Primate Central System Function. Technical report prepared for the New York State Power Lines Project. Albany, NY: Wadsworth Laboratories (E297), Empire State Plaza.

42. Wilson, B. W., L. E. Anderson, D. I. Hilton, and R. D. Phillips. 1981. Chronic exposure to 60-Hz electric fields: Effects on pineal function in the rat. Bioelectromagnetics 2: 371-380. [Erratum: Bioelectromagnetics; 4: 293 (1983)]. [PubMed]

43. Lerchl, A., K. O. Nonaka, K. A. Stokkan, and R. J. Reiter. 1990. Marked rapid alterations in nocturnal pineal serotonin metabolism in mice and rats exposed to weak intermittent magnetic fields. Biochem. Biophys. Res. Comm. 169:102-108. [PubMed]

44.
Tamarkin, L., C. J. Baird, and O. F. Almeida. 1985. Melatonin: A coordinating signal for mammalian reproduction. Science 227:714-720. [PubMed]

45.
Blask, D., and S. Hill. 1986. Effects of melatonin on cancer: Studies on MCF-7 human breast cancer cells in culture. J. Neural Transm. (Suppl.) 21:433-449. [PubMed]

46.
Stevens, R. G. 1987. Electric power use and breast cancer: A hypothesis. Am. J. Epidemiol. 125:556-561. [PubMed]

47.
Roberts, N. J. Jr., S.-T. Lu, and S. M. Michaelson. 1983. Human leukocyte radiation. Science 220:318-320. [PubMed]

48.
Roberts, N. J. Jr., S. M. Michaelson, and S.-T. Lu. 1984. Exposure of human mononuclear leukocytes to microwave energy pulse modulated at 16 or 60 Hz. IEEE Trans. Microwave Theory Tech. MTT-32: 803-807.

49.
Smialowicz, R. J., M. M. Riddle, P. L. Brugnolotti, J. M. Sperrazza, and J. B. Kinn. 1979. Evaluation of lymphocyte function in mice exposed to 2450 MHz (CW) microwaves. Pp. 122-152 in Electromagnetic Fields in Biological Systems, S. S. Stuchly, editor. , ed.

Edmonton, Canada: International Microwave Power Institute.

50.
Yang, H. K., C. A. Cain, J. Lockwood, and W. A. F. Tompkins. 1983. Effects of microwave exposure on the hamster immune system. I. Natural killer cell activity. Bioelectromagnetics 4:123-139. [PubMed]

51.
Rama Rao, G., C. A. Cain, J. Lockwood, and W. A. F. Tompkins. 1983. Effects of microwave exposure on the hamster immune system. II. Peritoneal macrophage function. Bioelectromagnetics 4:141-155. [PubMed]

52.
Liburdy, R. P. 1979. Radiofrequency radiation alters the immune system: Modification of T-and B-lymphocyte levels and cell-mediated immunocompetence by hyperthermic radiation. Radiat, Res. 77:34-46. [PubMed]

53.
Liburdy, R. P. 1980. Radiofrequency radiation alters the immune system. II. Modulation of in vivo lymphocyte circulation. Radiat. Res. 83:63-73. [PubMed]

54.
Smialowicz, R. J. 1985. Hematologic and immunologic effects of extremely low frequency electromagnetic fields. Pp. 203-225 in Biological and Human Health Effects of Extremely Low Frequency Electromagnetic Fields. Arlington, VA: American Institute of Biological Sciences.

55.
Conti, P., G. E. Gigante, M. G. Cifone, E. Alese, G. Ianni, M. Reale, and P. U. Angeletti. 1983. Reduced mitogenic stimulation of human lymphocytes by extremely low frequency electromagnetic fields. Fed. Europ. Biochem. Soc. (FEBS) 162:156-160. [PubMed]
56.
Conti, P., G. E. Gigante, M. G. Cifone, E. Alese, C. Fieschi, M. Bologna, and P. U. Angeletti. 1986. Mitogen dose-dependent effect of weak pulsed electromagnetic field on lymphocyte blastogenesis. Fed. Europ. Biochem. Soc. (FEBS) 199:130-134. [PubMed]
57.
Lyle, D. B., R. D. Ayotte, A. R. Sheppard, and W. R. Adey. 1988. Suppression of T-lymphocyte cytotoxicity following exposure to 60-Hz sinusoidal electric fields. Bioelectromagnetics 9:303-313. [PubMed]
58.
Winters, W. D. 1987. Biological Functions of Immunologically Reactive Human and Canine Cells Influenced by In Vitro Exposure to 60-Hz Electric and Magnetic Fields. Technical report prepared for the New York State Power Lines Project. Albany, NY: Wadsworth Laboratories (E-297), Empire State Plaza.
59.
Smialowicz, R. J. 1984. Hematologic and immunologic effects. Pp. 5.13-5.28 in Biological Effects of Radiofrequency Radiation, J. A. Elder, editor, and D. F. Cahill, editor. , eds. U.S.

Environmental Protection Agency Report No. EPA-600/8-83-026F. Health Effects Research Laboratory. Research Triangle Park, NC: United States Environmental Protection Agency.
60.
McRee, D. I., M. J. Galvin, and C. L. Mitchell. 1988. Microwave effects on the cardiovascular system: A model for studying the responsivity of the automatic nervous system to microwaves. Pp. 153-177 in Electromagnetic Fields and Neurobehavioral Function, M. E. O'Connor, editor, and R. H. Lovely, editor. , eds. New York, NY: Alan R. Liss. [PubMed]
61.
Liburdy, R. P. 1977. Effects of radiofrequency radiation on inflammation. Radio Sci. 12:179-183.
62.
Huang, A. T.-F., N. G. Mold. 1980. Immunologic and hematopoietic alterations by 2450-MHz electromagnetic radiation. Bioelectromagnetics 1:77-87. [PubMed]
63.
Ragan, H. A., R. D. Phillips, R. L. Buschbom, R. H. Busch, and J. E. Morris. 1983. Hematologic and immunologic effects of pulsed microwaves in mice. Bioelectromagnetics 4:383-396. [PubMed]
64.
Phillips, R. D., E. L. Hunt, R. D. Castro, and N. W. King. 1975. Thermoregulatory, metabolic, and cardiovascular responses of rats to microwaves. J. Appl. Physiol. 38:630-635. [PubMed]
65.

Chou, C.-K., K.-C. Yee, and A. W. Guy. 1980. Microwave radiation and heart-beat rate of rabbits. J. Microwave Power 15:87-93. [PubMed]

66.
Tenforde, T. S. 1986. Interaction of ELF magnetic fields with living matter. Pp. 197-225 in Handbook of Biological Effects of Electromagnetic Fields, C. Polk, editor, and E. Postow, editor. , eds. Boca Raton, FL: CRC Press.

67.
Hilton, D. I., and R. D. Phillips. 1981. Growth and metabolism of rodents exposed to 60-Hz electric fields.Bioelectromagnetics 2:381-390. [PubMed]

68.
Hauf, R. 1985. Hematological and biochemical effects of ELF fields in man: Laboratory experiments. Pp. 525-537 in Biological Effects and Dosimetry of Static and ELF Electromagnetic Fields, M. Grandolfo, editor, S. M. Michaelson, editor, and A. Rindi, editor. , eds. New York, NY: Plenum Press.

69.
Sander, R., J. Brinkmann, B. Kuhne. 1982. Laboratory studies on animals and human beings exposed to 50 Hz electric and magnetic fields. In Proc. Int. Conf. on Large High Voltage Electr. Syst., Paper No. 36-01 (Paris, France, Sept. 1982).

70.
Prausnitz, S., C. Susskind, and P. O. Vogelhut. 1962. Effects of chronic microwave irradiation on mice. I.R.E. Trans. Biomed. Electron. 9:104-108. [PubMed]

71.
Heynick, L. N. 1987. Critique of the literature on bioeffects of radiofrequency radiation: a comprehensive review pertinent to Air Force operations. USAFSAM-TR-87-3.
72.
Roberts, N. J., Jr., and S. M. Michaelson. 1983. Microwaves and neoplasia in mice: Analysis of a reported risk.Health Phys. 44:430-433. [PubMed]
73.
Spalding, J. F., R. W. Freyman, and L. M. Holland. 1971. Effects of 800-MHz electromagnetic radiation on body weight, activity, hematopoiesis, and life span in mice. Health Phys. 20:421-424. [PubMed]
74.
Kunz, L. L., R. B. Johnson, D. Thompson, J. Crowley, C.-K. Chou, and A. W. Guy. 1985. Effects of long-term low-level longevity, cause of death and histopathological findings, University of Washington. USAMSAM-TR-85-11-8.
75.
Szmigielski, S., A. Szudznski, A. Pietraszek, M. Bielec, M. Janiak, and J. K. Wrembel. 1982. Accelerated development of spontaneous and benzopyrene-induced skin cancer in mice exposed to 2,450-MHz microwave
radiation. Bioelectromagnetics 3:179-191. [PubMed]
76.
Santini, R., P. Hosni, P. Deschaux, and H. Pacheco. 1988. B16 melanoma development in black mice

exposed to low-level microwave radiation. Bioelectromagnetics 9:105-107. [PubMed]
77.
Roszkowski, M., J. K. Wrembel, K. Roszkowski, M. Janiak, and S. Szmigielski. 1980. Does whole-body hyperthermia therapy involve participation of the immune system? Natl. J. Cancer 25:289-292. [PubMed]
78.
Preskorn, S. H., W. D. Edwards, and D. R. Justesen. 1978. Retarded tumor growth and greater longevity in mice after fetal irradiation by 2,450-MHz microwaves. J. Surgical. Oncol. 10:483-492. [PubMed]
79.
McLean, J.R.N., M.A. Stuchly, R.E.J. Mitchell, D. Wilkinson, H. Yang, M. Goddard, D.W. Lecuyer, M. Schunk, E. Callary, and D. Morrison. 1991. Cancer promotion in a mouse-skin model by a 60-Hz magnetic field: II. Tumor development and immune response. Bioelectromagnetics 12:273-287. [PubMed]
80.
Beniashvili, D. Sh., V. G. Bilanishvili, M. Z. Menabde. 1991. Low-frequency electromagnetic radiation enhances the induction of rat mammary tumors by nitrosomethyl urea. Cancer Letters 61:75-79. [PubMed]

References (III)
References
1. Apel K, Hirt H. REACTIVE OXYGEN SPECIES: Metabolism, Oxidative Stress, and Signal Transduction. Annual Review of Plant Biology. 2004;55:373–399. [PubMed] [Google Scholar]
2. Dickinson BC, Chang CJ. Chemistry and biology of reactive oxygen species in signaling or stress responses. Nat Chem Biol. 2011;7:504–511. [PMC free article] [PubMed] [Google Scholar]
3. COOKE MS, EVANS MD, DIZDAROGLU M, LUNEC J. Oxidative DNA damage: mechanisms, mutation, and disease. The FASEB Journal. 2003;17:1195–1214. [PubMed] [Google Scholar]
4. Miao L, St.Clair DK. Regulation of superoxide dismutase genes: Implications in disease. Free Radical Biology and Medicine. 2009;47:344–356. [PMC free article] [PubMed] [Google Scholar]
5. Sturtz LA, Diekert K, Jensen LT, Lill R, Culotta VC. A Fraction of Yeast Cu,Zn-Superoxide Dismutase and Its Metallochaperone, CCS, Localize to the Intermembrane Space of Mitochondria: A PHYSIOLOGICAL ROLE FOR SOD1 IN GUARDING AGAINST MITOCHONDRIAL OXIDATIVE DAMAGE. Journal of Biological

Chemistry. 2001;276:38084-38089. [PubMed] [Google Scholar]
6. Bruijn LI, Miller TM, Cleveland DW. UNRAVELING THE MECHANISMS INVOLVED IN MOTOR NEURON DEGENERATION IN ALS. Annual Review of Neuroscience. 2004;27:723-749. [PubMed][Google Scholar]
7. Valentine JS, Doucette PA, Zittin Potter S. COPPER-ZINC SUPEROXIDE DISMUTASE AND AMYOTROPHIC LATERAL SCLEROSIS. Annual Review of Biochemistry. 2005;74:563-593. [PubMed][Google Scholar]
8. Muller FL, Lustgarten MS, Jang Y, Richardson A, Van Remmen H. Trends in oxidative aging theories.Free Radical Biology and Medicine. 2007;43:477-503. [PubMed] [Google Scholar]
9. Elchuri S, et al. CuZnSOD deficiency leads to persistent and widespread oxidative damage and hepatocarcinogenesis later in life. Oncogene. 2004;24:367-380. [PubMed] [Google Scholar]
10. Ayer A, et al. A Genome-Wide Screen in Yeast Identifies Specific Oxidative Stress Genes Required for the Maintenance of Sub-Cellular Redox Homeostasis. PLoS ONE. 2012;7:e44278. [PMC free article][PubMed] [Google Scholar]
11. Cressman DE, O'Connor WJ, Greer SF, Zhu X-S, Ting JP-Y. Mechanisms of Nuclear Import and Export That Control the Subcellular Localization of Class II Transactivator. The Journal of

Immunology.2001;167:3626–3634. [PubMed] [Google Scholar]
12. Kuge S, Toda T, Iizuka N, Nomoto A. Crm1 (XpoI) dependent nuclear export of the budding yeast transcription factor yAP-1 is sensitive to oxidative stress. Genes to Cells. 1998;3:521–532. [PubMed][Google Scholar]
13. Wen W, Meinkotht JL, Tsien RY, Taylor SS. Identification of a signal for rapid export of proteins from the nucleus. Cell. 1995;82:463–473. [PubMed] [Google Scholar]
14. Collins A. The comet assay for DNA damage and repair. Mol Biotechnol. 2004;26:249–261. [PubMed][Google Scholar]
15. Miloshev G, Mihaylov I, Anachkova B. Application of the single cell gel electrophoresis on yeast cells.Mutation Research/Genetic Toxicology and Environmental Mutagenesis. 2002;513:69–74. [PubMed][Google Scholar]
16. Guo Z, Kozlov S, Lavin MF, Person MD, Paull TT. ATM Activation by Oxidative Stress. Science.2010;330:517–521. [PubMed] [Google Scholar]
17. Carter CD, Kitchen LE, Au W-C, Babic CM, Basrai MA. Loss of SOD1 and LYS7 Sensitizes Saccharomyces cerevisiae to Hydroxyurea and DNA Damage Agents and Downregulates MEC1 Pathway Effectors. Molecular and Cellular Biology. 2005;25:10273–10285. [PMC free article] [PubMed][Google Scholar]

18. Ho Y, et al. Systematic identification of protein complexes in Saccharomyces cerevisiae by mass spectrometry. Nature. 2002;415:180–183. [PubMed] [Google Scholar]

19. Zhou Z, Elledge SJ. DUN1 encodes a protein kinase that controls the DNA damage response in yeast. Cell. 1993;75:1119–1127. [PubMed] [Google Scholar]

20. Zhao X, Rothstein R. The Dun1 checkpoint kinase phosphorylates and regulates the ribonucleotide reductase inhibitor Sml1. Proceedings of the National Academy of Sciences. 2002;99:3746–3751. [PMC free article] [PubMed] [Google Scholar]

21. Olsen JV, et al. Quantitative Phosphoproteomics Reveals Widespread Full Phosphorylation Site Occupancy During Mitosis. Sci. Signal. 2010;3 ra3- [PubMed] [Google Scholar]

22. Wilcox KC, et al. Modifications of Superoxide Dismutase (SOD1) in Human Erythrocytes: A POSSIBLE ROLE IN AMYOTROPHIC LATERAL SCLEROSIS. Journal of Biological Chemistry.2009;284:13940–13947. [PMC free article] [PubMed] [Google Scholar]

23. Chi A, et al. Analysis of phosphorylation sites on proteins from Saccharomyces cerevisiae by electron transfer dissociation (ETD) mass spectrometry. Proceedings of the National Academy of Sciences.2007;104:2193–2198. [PMC free article] [PubMed] [Google Scholar]

24. Uchiki T, Dice LT, Hettich RL, Dealwis C. Identification of Phosphorylation Sites on the Yeast

Ribonucleotide Reductase Inhibitor Sml1. Journal of Biological Chemistry. 2004;279:11293–11303.[PubMed] [Google Scholar]

25. Sanchez Y, Zhou Z, Huang M, Kemp BE, Elledge SJ. In: Methods in Enzymology. Dunphy William G, editor. Vol. 283. Academic Press; 1997. pp. 399–410. [Google Scholar]

26. Gasch AP, et al. Genomic Expression Programs in the Response of Yeast Cells to Environmental Changes. Molecular Biology of the Cell. 2000;11:4241–4257. [PMC free article] [PubMed][Google Scholar]

27. Reddi Amit R, Culotta Valeria C. SOD1 Integrates Signals from Oxygen and Glucose to Repress Respiration. Cell. 2013;152:224–235. [PMC free article] [PubMed] [Google Scholar]

28. Wei Y, Tsang C, Zheng X. Mechanisms of regulation of RNA polymerase III-dependent transcription by TORC1. EMBO J. 2009;28:2220–2230. [PMC free article] [PubMed] [Google Scholar]

29. Alabert C, Bianco J, Pasero P. Differential regulation of homologous recombination at DNA breaks and replication forks by the Mrc1 branch of the S-phase checkpoint. EMBO J. 2009;28:1131–1141.[PMC free article] [PubMed] [Google Scholar]

30. Castro F, Mariani D, Panek A, Eleutherio E, Pereira M. Cytotoxicity mechanism of two naphthoquinones (menadione and plumbagin) in Saccharomyces cerevisiae. PLoS One. 2008;3:e3999.[PMC free article] [PubMed] [Google Scholar]

31. Gałgańska H, et al. Viability of Saccharomyces cerevisiae cells following exposure to H2O2 and protective effect of minocycline depend on the presence of VDAC. European Journal of Pharmacology.2010;643:42–47. [PubMed] [Google Scholar]
32. Giannattasio M, Lazzaro F, Longhese M, Plevani P, Muzi-Falconi M. Physical and functional interactions between nucleotide excision repair and DNA damage checkpoint. EMBO J. 2004;23:429–438.[PMC free article] [PubMed] [Google Scholar]
33. Jiang YW, Kang CM. Induction of S. cerevisiae Filamentous Differentiation by Slowed DNA Synthesis Involves Mec1, Rad53 and Swe1 Checkpoint Proteins. Mol. Biol. Cell. 2003;14:5116–5124.[PMC free article] [PubMed] [Google Scholar]
34. Somwar R, et al. Superoxide dismutase 1 (SOD1) is a target for a small molecule identified in a screen for inhibitors of the growth of lung adenocarcinoma cell lines. Proceedings of the National Academy of Sciences. 2011;108:16375–16380. [PMC free article] [PubMed] [Google Scholar]
35. Vassallo N, Galea D, Bannister W, Balzan R. Stimulation of yeast 3-phosphoglycerate kinase gene promoter by paraquat. Biochem Biophys Res Commun. 2000;270:1036–1040. [PubMed] [Google Scholar]
36. Tsang CK, Zheng XFS. Opposing Role of Condensin and Radiation-sensitive Gene RAD52 in Ribosomal DNA Stability Regulation. J.Biol.

Chem. 2009;284:21908–21919. [PMC free article] [PubMed][Google Scholar]

37. Liu X, Zheng XFS. Endoplasmic Reticulum and Golgi Localization Sequences for Mammalian Target of Rapamycin. Molecular Biology of the Cell. 2007;18:1073–1082. [PMC free article] [PubMed][Google Scholar]

38. Ziv Y, et al. Recombinant ATM protein complements the cellular A-T phenotype. Oncogene.1997;15:159–167. [PubMed] [Google Scholar]

39. Weydert CJ, Cullen JJ. Measurement of superoxide dismutase, catalase, and glutathione peroxidase in cultured cells and tissue. Nat Protocols. 2010;5:51–66. [PMC free article] [PubMed] [Google Scholar]

40. Azevedo F, Marques F, Fokt H, Oliveira R, Johansson B. Measuring oxidative DNA damage and DNA repair using the yeast comet assay. Yeast. 2011;28:55–61. [PubMed] [Google Scholar]

41. Madeo F, Fröhlich E, Fröhlich K-U. A Yeast Mutant Showing Diagnostic Markers of Early and Late Apoptosis. The Journal of Cell Biology. 1997;139:729–734. [PMC free article] [PubMed] [Google Scholar]

42. Collart MA, Oliviero S. Current Protocols in Molecular Biology. John Wiley & Sons, Inc; 2001.[Google Scholar]

43. Causton HC, et al. Remodeling of Yeast Genome Expression in Response to Environmental

Changes.Molecular Biology of the Cell. 2001;12:323–337. [PMC free article] [PubMed] [Google Scholar]

44. Nolan T, Hands RE, Bustin SA. Quantification of mRNA using real-time RT-PCR. Nat. Protocols.2006;1:1559–1582. [PubMed] [Google Scholar]

45. Li H, Tsang CK, Watkins M, Bertram PG, Zheng XFS. Nutrient regulates Tor1 nuclear localization and association with rDNA promoter. Nature. 2006;442:1058–1061. [PubMed] [Google Scholar]

46. Tsang CK, Bertram PG, Ai W, Drenan R, Zheng XFS. Chromatin-mediated regulation of nucleolar structure and RNA Pol I localization by TOR. The EMBO Journal. 2003;22:6045–6056. [PMC free article][PubMed] [Google Scholar]

Formats:

Article

|

PubReader

|

ePub (beta)

|

PDF (2.3M)

|

Citation

Share

 Facebook

 Twitter

 Google+

Save items

https://www.ncbi.nlm.nih.gov/pmc/articles/PMC4678626/
Add to FavoritesView more options
Similar articles in PubMed
https://www.ncbi.nlm.nih.gov/pmc/articles/PMC4678626/
Loss of SOD1 and LYS7 sensitizes Saccharomyces cerevisiae to hydroxyurea and DNA damage agents and downregulates MEC1 pathway effectors.[Mol Cell Biol. 2005]
Overexpression of human SOD1 in VDAC1-less yeast restores mitochondrial functionality modulating beta-barrel outer membrane protein genes.[Biochim Biophys Acta. 2016]
PSK1 regulates expression of SOD1 involved in oxidative stress tolerance in yeast.[FEMS Microbiol Lett. 2014]
Unraveling new functions of superoxide dismutase using yeast model system: Beyond its conventional role in superoxide radical scavenging.[J Microbiol. 2017]
Hydrogen peroxide sensing and signaling by protein kinases in the cardiovascular system.[Antioxid Redox Signal. 2013]
See reviews...See all...
Cited by other articles in PMC
https://www.ncbi.nlm.nih.gov/pmc/articles/PMC4678626/
ROS in cancer therapy: the bright side of the moon

Nuclear factor-kB and nitric oxide synthases in red blood cells: Good or bad in obesity? A preliminary study[European Journal of Histochemi...]
Endoplasmic reticulum stress differentially inhibits endoplasmic reticulum and inner nuclear membrane protein quality control degradation pathways[The Journal of Biological Chem...]
On the epigenetic role of guanosine oxidation[Redox Biology. 2019]
Characterization of the activity, aggregation, and toxicity of heterodimers of WT and ALS-associated mutant Sod1[Proceedings of the National Ac...]
See all...
Links
https://www.ncbi.nlm.nih.gov/pmc/articles/PMC4678626/
BioProject
Compound
Gene
GEO DataSets
GEO Profiles
MedGen
Nucleotide
Pathways + GO
PubMed
Taxonomy
Recent Activity
https://www.ncbi.nlm.nih.gov/pmc/articles/PMC4678626/
ClearTurn Off

Superoxide dismutase 1 acts as a nuclear transcription factor to regulate oxidat...
Superoxide dismutase 1 acts as a nuclear transcription factor to regulate oxidative stress resistance
NIHPA Author Manuscripts. 2014; 5()3446

ROS Function in Redox Signaling and Oxidative Stress
ROS Function in Redox Signaling and Oxidative Stress
NIHPA Author Manuscripts. 2014 May 19; 24(10)R453

A Review of Coronavirus Disease-2019 (COVID-19).
A Review of Coronavirus Disease-2019 (COVID-19).
Indian J Pediatr. 2020 Apr;87(4):281-286. doi: 10.1007/s12098-020-03263-6. Epub 2020 Mar 13.
PubMed

Effects of Electromagnetic Fields on Organs and Tissues - Assessment of the Poss...
Effects of Electromagnetic Fields on Organs and Tissues - Assessment of the Possible Health Effects of Ground Wave Emergency Network

Intravenous superoxide dismutase as a protective agent to prevent impairment of ...
Intravenous superoxide dismutase as a protective agent to prevent impairment of lung function induced by high tidal volume ventilation
Nature Public Health Emergency Collection. 2017; 17()

See more...

A genome-wide screen in yeast identifies specific oxidative stress genes required for the maintenance of sub-cellular redox homeostasis.[PLoS One. 2012]
Mechanisms of nuclear import and export that control the subcellular localization of class II transactivator.[J Immunol. 2001]
Crm1 (XpoI) dependent nuclear export of the budding yeast transcription factor yAP-1 is sensitive to oxidative stress.[Genes Cells. 1998]
Identification of a signal for rapid export of proteins from the nucleus.[Cell. 1995]
Review The comet assay for DNA damage and repair: principles, applications, and limitations.[Mol Biotechnol. 2004]
Application of the single cell gel electrophoresis on yeast cells.[Mutat Res. 2002]
ATM activation by oxidative stress.[Science. 2010]
Loss of SOD1 and LYS7 sensitizes Saccharomyces cerevisiae to hydroxyurea and DNA damage agents and downregulates MEC1 pathway effectors.[Mol Cell Biol. 2005]
Systematic identification of protein complexes in Saccharomyces cerevisiae by mass spectrometry.[Nature. 2002]
DUN1 encodes a protein kinase that controls the DNA damage response in yeast.[Cell. 1993]
The Dun1 checkpoint kinase phosphorylates and regulates the ribonucleotide reductase inhibitor Sml1.[Proc Natl Acad Sci U S A. 2002]

Quantitative phosphoproteomics reveals widespread full phosphorylation site occupancy during mitosis.[Sci Signal. 2010]
Modifications of superoxide dismutase (SOD1) in human erythrocytes: a possible role in amyotrophic lateral sclerosis.[J Biol Chem. 2009]
Analysis of phosphorylation sites on proteins from Saccharomyces cerevisiae by electron transfer dissociation (ETD) mass spectrometry.[Proc Natl Acad Sci U S A. 2007]
Identification of phosphorylation sites on the yeast ribonucleotide reductase inhibitor Sml1.[J Biol Chem. 2004]
Genomic expression programs in the response of yeast cells to environmental changes.[Mol Biol Cell. 2000]
Quantitative phosphoproteomics reveals widespread full phosphorylation site occupancy during mitosis.[Sci Signal. 2010]
Modifications of superoxide dismutase (SOD1) in human erythrocytes: a possible role in amyotrophic lateral sclerosis.[J Biol Chem. 2009]
ATM activation by oxidative stress.[Science. 2010]
SOD1 integrates signals from oxygen and glucose to repress respiration.[Cell. 2013]
Mechanisms of regulation of RNA polymerase III-dependent transcription by TORC1.[EMBO J. 2009]
Differential regulation of homologous recombination at DNA breaks and replication forks by the Mrc1 branch of the S-phase checkpoint.[EMBO J. 2009]

Stimulation of yeast 3-phosphoglycerate kinase gene promoter by paraquat.[Biochem Biophys Res Commun. 2000]
Opposing role of condensin and radiation-sensitive gene RAD52 in ribosomal DNA stability regulation.[J Biol Chem. 2009]
Endoplasmic reticulum and Golgi localization sequences for mammalian target of rapamycin.[Mol Biol Cell. 2007]
Recombinant ATM protein complements the cellular A-T phenotype.[Oncogene. 1997]
Measurement of superoxide dismutase, catalase and glutathione peroxidase in cultured cells and tissue.[Nat Protoc. 2010]
The Dun1 checkpoint kinase phosphorylates and regulates the ribonucleotide reductase inhibitor Sml1.[Proc Natl Acad Sci U S A. 2002]
Measuring oxidative DNA damage and DNA repair using the yeast comet assay.[Yeast. 2011]
A yeast mutant showing diagnostic markers of early and late apoptosis.[J Cell Biol. 1997]
Genomic expression programs in the response of yeast cells to environmental changes.[Mol Biol Cell. 2000]
Remodeling of yeast genome expression in response to environmental changes.[Mol Biol Cell. 2001]
Quantification of mRNA using real-time RT-PCR.[Nat Protoc. 2006]
A yeast mutant showing diagnostic markers of early and late apoptosis.[J Cell Biol. 1997]

Nutrient regulates Tor1 nuclear localization and association with rDNA promoter.[Nature. 2006]
Chromatin-mediated regulation of nucleolar structure and RNA Pol I localization by TOR.[EMBO J. 2003]
Support CenterSupport Center

References (IV)
References
1. Acute Respiratory Distress Syndrome Network Ventilation with lower tidal volumes as compared with traditional tidal volumes for acute lung injury and the acute respiratory distress syndrome. N Engl J Med.2000;342(18):1301–1308. doi: 10.1056/NEJM200005043421801. [PubMed] [CrossRef] [Google Scholar]
2. Andersen GN, Nilsson K, Pourazar J, Hackett TL, Kazzam E, Blomberg A, Waldenstrom A, Warner J, Rantapaa-Dahlqvist S, Mincheva-Nilsson L, Sandstrom T. Bronchoalveolar matrix metalloproteinase 9 relates to restrictive lung function impairment in systemic sclerosis. Respir Med. 2007;101(10):2199–2206. doi: 10.1016/j.rmed.2007.04.019. [PubMed] [CrossRef] [Google Scholar]
3. Barnes PJ. Mediators of chronic obstructive pulmonary disease. Pharmacol Rev. 2004;56(4):515–548. doi: 10.1124/pr.56.4.2. [PubMed] [CrossRef] [Google Scholar]
4. Bridges JP, Davis HW, Damodarasamy M, Kuroki Y, Howles G, Hui DY, McCormack FX. Pulmonary

surfactant proteins a and D are potent endogenous inhibitors of lipid peroxidation and oxidative cellular injury. J Biol Chem. 2000;275(49):38848–38855. doi: 10.1074/jbc.M005322200. [PubMed] [CrossRef][Google Scholar]
5. Chiang CH, Pai HI, Liu SL. Ventilator-induced lung injury (VILI) promotes ischemia/reperfusion lung injury (I/R) and NF-kappaB antibody attenuates both
injuries. Resuscitation. 2008;79(1):147–154. doi: 10.1016/j.resuscitation.2008.02.028. [PubMed] [CrossRef] [Google Scholar]
6. Chiang YM, Lo CP, Chen YP, Wang SY, Yang NS, Kuo YH, Shyur LF. Ethyl caffeate suppresses NF-kappaB activation and its downstream inflammatory mediators, iNOS, COX-2, and PGE2 in vitro or in mouse skin. Br J Pharmacol. 2005;146(3):352–363. doi: 10.1038/sj.bjp.0706343. [PMC free article][PubMed] [CrossRef] [Google Scholar]
7. Choi IW, Sun K, Kim YS, Ko HM, Im SY, Kim JH, You HJ, Lee YC, Lee JH, Park YM, Lee HK. TNF-alpha induces the late-phase airway hyperresponsiveness and airway inflammation through cytosolic phospholipase a(2) activation. J Allergy Clin Immunol. 2005;116(3):537–543. doi: 10.1016/j.jaci.2005.05.034. [PubMed] [CrossRef] [Google Scholar]
8. Cook-Mills JM, Marchese ME, Abdala-Valencia H. Vascular cell adhesion molecule-1 expression and signaling during disease: regulation by reactive oxygen species and antioxidants. Antioxid Redox

Signal.2011;15(6):1607–1638. doi: 10.1089/ars.2010.3522. [PMC free article] [PubMed] [CrossRef][Google Scholar]

9. Corry DB, Kiss A, Song LZ, Song L, Xu J, Lee SH, Werb Z, Kheradmand F. Overlapping and independent contributions of MMP2 and MMP9 to lung allergic inflammatory cell egression through decreased CC chemokines. FASEB J. 2004;18(9):995–997. [PMC free article] [PubMed] [Google Scholar]

10. D'Angelo E, Pecchiari M, Baraggia P, Saetta M, Balestro E, Milic-Emili J. Low-volume ventilation causes peripheral airway injury and increased airway resistance in normal rabbits. J Appl Physiol.2002;92(3):949–956. doi: 10.1152/japplphysiol.00776.2001. [PubMed] [CrossRef] [Google Scholar]

11. Davidovich N, DiPaolo BC, Lawrence GG, Chhour P, Yehya N, Margulies SS. Cyclic stretch-induced oxidative stress increases pulmonary alveolar epithelial permeability. Am J Respir Cell Mol Biol.2013;49(1):156–164. doi: 10.1165/rcmb.2012-0252OC. [PMC free article] [PubMed] [CrossRef][Google Scholar]

12. de Haan JB, Cristiano F, Iannello R, Bladier C, Kelner MJ, Kola I. Elevation in the ratio of Cu/Zn-superoxide dismutase to glutathione peroxidase activity induces features of cellular senescence and this effect is mediated by hydrogen peroxide. Hum Mol Genet. 1996;5(2):283–292. doi: 10.1093/hmg/5.2.283.[PubMed] [CrossRef] [Google Scholar]

13. de Haan JB, Cristiano F, Iannello RC, Kola I. Cu/Zn-superoxide dismutase and glutathione peroxidase during aging. Biochem Mol Biol Int. 1995;35(6):1281–1297. [PubMed] [Google Scholar]
14. Fagan KA, Tyler RC, Sato K, Fouty BW, Morris KG, Jr, Huang PL, McMurtry IF, Rodman DM. Relative contributions of endothelial, inducible, and neuronal NOS to tone in the murine pulmonary circulation. Am J Phys. 1999;277(3 Pt 1):L472–L478. [PubMed] [Google Scholar]
15. Frank JA, Wray CM, McAuley DF, Schwendener R, Matthay MA. Alveolar macrophages contribute to alveolar barrier dysfunction in ventilator-induced lung injury. Am J Physiol Lung Cell Mol Physiol.2006;291(6):L1191–L1198. doi: 10.1152/ajplung.00055.2006. [PubMed] [CrossRef] [Google Scholar]
16. Frostell CG, Blomqvist H, Hedenstierna G, Lundberg J, Zapol WM. Inhaled nitric oxide selectively reverses human hypoxic pulmonary vasoconstriction without causing systemic vasodilation.Anesthesiology. 1993;78(3):427–435. doi: 10.1097/00000542-199303000-00005. [PubMed] [CrossRef][Google Scholar]
17. Fukai T, Ushio-Fukai M. Superoxide dismutases: role in redox signaling, vascular function, and diseases. Antioxid Redox Signal. 2011;15(6):1583–1606. doi: 10.1089/ars.2011.3999. [PMC free article][PubMed] [CrossRef] [Google Scholar]
18. Gajic O, Dara SI, Mendez JL, Adesanya AO, Festic E, Caples SM, Rana R, St Sauver JL, Lymp JF, Afessa

B, Hubmayr RD. Ventilator-associated lung injury in patients without acute lung injury at the onset of mechanical ventilation. Crit Care Med. 2004;32(9):1817–1824. doi: 10.1097/01.CCM.0000133019.52531.30. [PubMed] [CrossRef] [Google Scholar]

19. Glosli H, Tronstad KJ, Wergedal H, Muller F, Svardal A, Aukrust P, Berge RK, Prydz H. Human TNF-alpha in transgenic mice induces differential changes in redox status and glutathione-regulating enzymes.FASEB J. 2002;16(11):1450–1452. [PubMed] [Google Scholar]

20. Guery BP, Welsh DA, Viget NB, Robriquet L, Fialdes P, Mason CM, Beaucaire G, Bagby GJ, Neviere R. Ventilation-induced lung injury is associated with an increase in gut permeability. Shock.2003;19(6):559–563. doi: 10.1097/01.shk.0000070738.34700.bf. [PubMed] [CrossRef] [Google Scholar]

21. Hampl V, Herget J. Role of nitric oxide in the pathogenesis of chronic pulmonary hypertension. Physiol Rev. 2000;80(4):1337–1372. [PubMed] [Google Scholar]

22. Hartshorn KL, Crouch E, White MR, Colamussi ML, Kakkanatt A, Tauber B, Shepherd V, Sastry KN. Pulmonary surfactant proteins a and D enhance neutrophil uptake of bacteria. Am J Phys. 1998;274(6 Pt 1):L958–L969. [PubMed] [Google Scholar]

23. He C, Murthy S, Ryan AJ, Carter B. Cu,Zn-SOD down-regulates MMP-9 expression via inhibition of

ERK. Am J Prepir Crit Care
Med. 2011;183:A2441. [Google Scholar]
24. Held HD, Boettcher S, Hamann L, Uhlig S. Ventilation-induced chemokine and cytokine release is associated with activation of nuclear factor-kappaB and is blocked by steroids. Am J Respir Crit Care Med.2001;163(3 Pt 1):711-716. doi: 10.1164/ajrccm.163.3.2003001. [PubMed] [CrossRef] [Google Scholar]
25. Herbein JF, Savov J, Wright JR. Binding and uptake of surfactant protein D by freshly isolated rat alveolar type II cells. Am J Physiol Lung Cell Mol Physiol. 2000;278(4):L830-L839. [PubMed][Google Scholar]
26. Hughes JM, Stringer RS, Black JL, Armour CL. The effects of tumour necrosis factor alpha on mediator release from human lung. Pulm Pharmacol. 1995;8(1):31-36. doi: 10.1006/pulp.1995.1004.[PubMed] [CrossRef] [Google Scholar]
27. Ischiropoulos H, Zhu L, Chen J, Tsai M, Martin JC, Smith CD, Beckman JS. Peroxynitrite-mediated tyrosine nitration catalyzed by superoxide dismutase. Arch Biochem Biophys. 1992;298(2):431-437. doi: 10.1016/0003-9861(92)90431-U. [PubMed] [CrossRef] [Google Scholar]
28. Jacobson JR, Birukov KG. Activation of NFkB and coagulation in lung injury by hyperoxia and excessive mechanical ventilation: one more reason "low and slow" is the way to go? Transl Res.2009;154(5):219-221. doi:

10.1016/j.trsl.2009.07.012. [PMC free article] [PubMed] [CrossRef][Google Scholar]
29. Janero DR. Malondialdehyde and thiobarbituric acid-reactivity as diagnostic indices of lipid peroxidation and peroxidative tissue injury. Free Radic Biol Med. 1990;9(6):515–540. doi: 10.1016/0891-5849(90)90131-2. [PubMed] [CrossRef] [Google Scholar]
30. Jiang L, Quarck R, Janssens S, Pokreisz P, Demedts M, Delcroix M. Effect of adenovirus-mediated gene transfer of nitric oxide synthase on vascular reactivity of rat isolated pulmonary arteries. Pflugers Arch. 2006;452(2):213–221. doi: 10.1007/s00424-005-0028-3. [PubMed] [CrossRef] [Google Scholar]
31. Jung O, Marklund SL, Geiger H, Pedrazzini T, Busse R, Brandes RP. Extracellular superoxide dismutase is a major determinant of nitric oxide bioavailability: in vivo and ex vivo evidence from ecSOD-deficient mice. Circ Res. 2003;93(7):622–629. doi: 10.1161/01.RES.0000092140.81594.A8. [PubMed] [CrossRef] [Google Scholar]
32. Khubchandani KR, Snyder JM. Surfactant protein a (SP-A): the alveolus and beyond. FASEB J.2001;15(1):59–69. doi: 10.1096/fj.00-0318rev. [PubMed] [CrossRef] [Google Scholar]
33. Kim JH, Suk MH, Yoon DW, Lee SH, Hur GY, Jung KH, Jeong HC, Lee SY, Lee SY, Suh IB, Shin C, Shim JJ, In KH, Yoo SH, Kang KH. Inhibition of matrix metalloproteinase-9 prevents neutrophilic inflammation in ventilator-induced lung injury. Am J

Physiol Lung Cell Mol Physiol. 2006;291(4): L580-L587. doi: 10.1152/ajplung.00270.2005. [PubMed] [CrossRef] [Google Scholar]

34. Kim KH, Lee JY, Kwun MJ, Choi JY, Han CW, Ha KT, Jeong SI, Jeong HS, Joo M. Therapeutic effect of Mahaenggamseok-tang on neutrophilic lung inflammation is associated with NF-κB suppression and Nrf2 activation. J Ethnopharmacol. 2016;192:486-95. [PubMed]

35. Ko YA, Yang MC, Huang HT, Hsu CM, Chen LW. NF-kappaB activation in myeloid cells mediates ventilator-induced lung injury. Respir Res. 2013;14:69. doi: 10.1186/1465-9921-14-69. [PMC free article][PubMed] [CrossRef] [Google Scholar]

36. Lawrence T. The nuclear factor NF-kappaB pathway in inflammation. Cold Spring Harb Perspect Biol.2009;1(6):a001651. doi: 10.1101/cshperspect.a001651. [PMC free article] [PubMed] [CrossRef][Google Scholar]

37. Lee IT, Yang CM. Inflammatory signalings involved in airway and pulmonary diseases. Mediat Inflamm. 2013;2013:791231. [PMC free article] [PubMed] [Google Scholar]

38. Lellouche F, Dionne S, Simard S, Bussieres J, Dagenais F. High tidal volumes in mechanically ventilated patients increase organ dysfunction after cardiac surgery. Anesthesiology. 2012;116(5):1072-1082. doi: 10.1097/ALN.0b013e3182522df5. [PubMed] [CrossRef] [Google Scholar]

39. Li H, Su X, Yan X, Wasserloos K, Chao W, Kaynar AM, Liu ZQ, Leikauf GD, Pitt BR, Zhang LM. Toll-

like receptor 4-myeloid differentiation factor 88 signaling contributes to ventilator-induced lung injury in mice. Anesthesiology. 2010;113(3):619–629. [PMC free article] [PubMed] [Google Scholar]

40. Lilly CM, Cody S, Zhao H, Landry K, Baker SP, McIlwaine J, Chandler MW, Irwin RS. Hospital mortality, length of stay, and preventable complications among critically ill patients before and after tele-ICU reengineering of critical care processes. JAMA. 2011;305(21):2175–83. [PubMed]

41. Lin SJ, Shyue SK, Hung YY, Chen YH, Ku HH, Chen JW, Tam KB, Chen YL. Superoxide dismutase inhibits the expression of vascular cell adhesion molecule-1 and intracellular cell adhesion molecule-1 induced by tumor necrosis factor-alpha in human endothelial cells through the JNK/p38 pathways.Arterioscler Thromb Vasc Biol. 2005;25(2):334–340. doi: 10.1161/01.ATV.0000152114.00114.d8.[PubMed] [CrossRef] [Google Scholar]

42. Lin SM, Lin HC, Lee KY, Huang CD, Liu CY, Wang CH, Kuo HP. Ventilator-induced injury augments interleukin-1beta production and neutrophil sequestration in lipopolysaccharide-treated lungs. Shock.2007;28(4):453–460. doi: 10.1097/shk.0b013e3180487fb5. [PubMed] [CrossRef] [Google Scholar]

43. Liu YY, Li LF, Yang CT, Lu KH, Huang CC, Kao KC, Chiou SH. Suppressing NF-kappaB and NKRF pathways by induced pluripotent stem cell therapy in mice with ventilator-induced lung injury. PLoS

One.2013;8(6):e66760. doi: 10.1371/journal.pone.0066760. [PMC free article] [PubMed] [CrossRef][Google Scholar]
44. Lopez-Alonso I, Aguirre A, Gonzalez-Lopez A, Fernandez AF, Amado-Rodriguez L, Astudillo A, Batalla-Solis E, Albaiceta GM. Impairment of autophagy decreases ventilator-induced lung injury by blockade of the NF-kappaB pathway. Am J Physiol Lung Cell Mol Physiol. 2013;304(12): L844–L852. doi: 10.1152/ajplung.00422.2012. [PubMed] [CrossRef] [Google Scholar]
45. Lundblad LK, Thompson-Figueroa J, Leclair T, Sullivan MJ, Poynter ME, Irvin CG, Bates JH. Tumor necrosis factor-alpha overexpression in lung disease: a single cause behind a complex phenotype. Am J Respir Crit Care Med. 2005;171(12):1363–1370. doi: 10.1164/rccm.200410-1349OC. [PMC free article][PubMed] [CrossRef] [Google Scholar]
46. Lynch SM, Frei B, Morrow JD, Roberts LJ, Xu A, Jackson T, Reyna R, Klevay LM, Vita JA, Keaney JF., Jr Vascular superoxide dismutase deficiency impairs endothelial vasodilator function through direct inactivation of nitric oxide and increased lipid peroxidation. Arterioscler Thromb Vasc Biol.1997;17(11):2975–2981. doi: 10.1161/01.ATV.17.11.2975. [PubMed] [CrossRef] [Google Scholar]
47. Madan T, Kishore U, Singh M, Strong P, Clark H, Hussain EM, Reid KB, Sarma PU. Surfactant proteins a and D protect mice against pulmonary hypersensitivity induced by Aspergillus fumigatus

antigens and allergens. J Clin Invest. 2001;107(4):467–475. doi: 10.1172/JCI10124. [PMC free article][PubMed] [CrossRef] [Google Scholar]
48. Malhotra A. Low-tidal-volume ventilation in the acute respiratory distress syndrome. N Engl J Med.2007;357(11):1113–1120. doi: 10.1056/NEJMct074213. [PMC free article] [PubMed] [CrossRef][Google Scholar]
49. Marberger H, Bartsch G, Huber W, Menander KB, Schulte TL. Orgotein: a new drug for the treatment of radiation cystitis. Curr Ther Res Clin Exp. 1975;18(3):466–475. [PubMed] [Google Scholar]
50. Marikovsky M, Ziv V, Nevo N, Harris-Cerruti C, Mahler O. Cu/Zn superoxide dismutase plays important role in immune response. J Immunol. 2003;170(6):2993–3001. doi: 10.4049/jimmunol.170.6.2993. [PubMed] [CrossRef] [Google Scholar]
51. Martinez-Caro L, Lorente JA, Marin-Corral J, Sanchez-Rodriguez C, Sanchez-Ferrer A, Nin N, Ferruelo A, de Paula M, Fernandez-Segoviano P, Barreiro E, Esteban A. Role of free radicals in vascular dysfunction induced by high tidal volume ventilation. Intensive Care Med. 2009;35(6):1110–1119. doi: 10.1007/s00134-009-1469-5. [PubMed] [CrossRef] [Google Scholar]
52. Maruscak AA, Vockeroth DW, Girardi B, Sheikh T, Possmayer F, Lewis JF, Veldhuizen RA. Alterations to surfactant precede physiological deterioration during high tidal volume ventilation. Am J Physiol Lung Cell Mol

Physiol. 2008;294(5):L974–L983. doi: 10.1152/ajplung.00528.2007. [PubMed] [CrossRef] [Google Scholar]
53. Mikawa K, Nishina K, Maekawa N, Obara H. Attenuation of hyperoxic lung injury in rabbits with superoxide dismutase: effects on inflammatory mediators. Acta Anaesthesiol Scand. 1995;39(3):317–322. doi: 10.1111/j.1399-6576.1995.tb04069.x. [PubMed] [CrossRef] [Google Scholar]
54. Minotti G, Aust SD. The role of iron in the initiation of lipid peroxidation. Chem Phys Lipids.1987;44(2–4):191–208. doi: 10.1016/0009-3084(87)90050-8. [PubMed] [CrossRef] [Google Scholar]
55. Mukhopadhyay S, Hoidal JR, Mukherjee TK. Role of TNFalpha in pulmonary pathophysiology. Respir Res. 2006;7:125. doi: 10.1186/1465-9921-7-125. [PMC free article] [PubMed] [CrossRef] [Google Scholar]
56. Nahar N, Shah H, Siu J, Colvin R, Bhaskaran M, Ranjan R, Wagner JD, Singhal PC. Dialysis membrane-induced neutrophil apoptosis is mediated through free radicals. Clin Nephrol. 2001;56(1):52–59. [PubMed] [Google Scholar]
57. Oury TD, Day BJ, Crapo JD. Extracellular superoxide dismutase: a regulator of nitric oxide bioavailability. Lab Investig. 1996;75(5):617–636. [PubMed] [Google Scholar]
58. Park SK, Dahmer MK, Quasney MW. MAPK and JAK-STAT signaling pathways are involved in the oxidative stress-induced decrease in expression of

surfactant protein genes. Cell Physiol Biochem.2012;30(2):334–346. doi: 10.1159/000339068. [PubMed] [CrossRef] [Google Scholar]
59. Peng X, Abdulnour RE, Sammani S, Ma SF, Han EJ, Hasan EJ, Tuder R, Garcia JG, Hassoun PM. Inducible nitric oxide synthase contributes to ventilator-induced lung injury. Am J Respir Crit Care Med.2005;172(4):470–479. doi: 10.1164/rccm.200411-1547OC. [PMC free article] [PubMed] [CrossRef][Google Scholar]
60. Pugin J, Dunn I, Jolliet P, Tassaux D, Magnenat JL, Nicod LP, Chevrolet JC. Activation of human macrophages by mechanical ventilation in vitro. Am J Phys. 1998;275(6 Pt 1): L1040–L1050. [PubMed][Google Scholar]
61. Quinn DA, Moufarrej RK, Volokhov A, Hales CA. Interactions of lung stretch, hyperoxia, and MIP-2 production in ventilator-induced lung injury. J Appl Physiol (1985) 2002;93(2):517–525. doi: 10.1152/japplphysiol.00570.2001. [PubMed] [CrossRef] [Google Scholar]
62. Rahman I. Oxidative stress in pathogenesis of chronic obstructive pulmonary disease: cellular and molecular mechanisms. Cell Biochem Biophys. 2005;43(1):167–188. doi: 10.1385/CBB:43:1:167.[PubMed] [CrossRef] [Google Scholar]
63. Ramnarine SI, Khawaja AM, Barnes PJ, Rogers DF. Nitric oxide inhibition of basal and neurogenic mucus secretion in ferret trachea in vitro. Br J

Pharmacol. 1996;118(4):998–1002. doi: 10.1111/j.1476-5381.1996.tb15498.x. [PMC free article] [PubMed] [CrossRef] [Google Scholar]
64. Reitsma S, Slaaf DW, Vink H, van Zandvoort MA, oude Egbrink MG. The endothelial glycocalyx: composition, functions, and visualization. Pflugers Arch. 2007;454(3):345–359. doi: 10.1007/s00424-007-0212-8. [PMC free article] [PubMed] [CrossRef] [Google Scholar]
65. Remels AH, Schrauwen P, Broekhuizen R, Willems J, Kersten S, Gosker HR, Schols AM. Peroxisome proliferator-activated receptor expression is reduced in skeletal muscle in COPD. Eur Respir J.2007;30(2):245–252. doi: 10.1183/09031936.00144106. [PubMed] [CrossRef] [Google Scholar]
66. Saputri RK, Setiawan B, Nugrahenny D, Kania N, Wahyuni ES, Widodo MA. The effects of Eucheuma Cottonii on alveolar macrophages and malondialdehyde levels in bronchoalveolar lavage fluid in chronically particulate matter 10 coal dust-exposed rats. Iran J Basic Med Sci. 2014;17(7):541–545.[PMC free article] [PubMed] [Google Scholar]
67. Sato A, Whitsett JA, Scheule RK, Ikegami M. Surfactant protein-d inhibits lung inflammation caused by ventilation in premature newborn lambs. Am J Respir Crit Care Med. 2010;181(10):1098–1105. doi: 10.1164/rccm.200912-1818OC. [PMC free article] [PubMed] [CrossRef] [Google Scholar]
68. Savla U, Sporn PH, Waters CM. Cyclic stretch of airway epithelium inhibits prostanoid synthesis. Am

J Phys. 1997;273(5 Pt 1):L1013–L1019. [PubMed] [Google Scholar]
69. Schock BC, Sweet DG, Ennis M, Warner JA, Young IS, Halliday HL. Oxidative stress and increased type-IV collagenase levels in bronchoalveolar lavage fluid from newborn babies. Pediatr Res.2001;50(1):29–33. doi: 10.1203/00006450-200107000-00008. [PubMed] [CrossRef] [Google Scholar]
70. Schunemann HJ, Muti P, Freudenheim JL, Armstrong D, Browne R, Klocke RA, Trevisan M. Oxidative stress and lung function. Am J Epidemiol. 1997;146(11):939–948. doi: 10.1093/oxfordjournals.aje.a009220. [PubMed] [CrossRef] [Google Scholar]
71. Segui J, Gil F, Gironella M, Alvarez M, Gimeno M, Coronel P, Closa D, Pique JM, Panes J. Down-regulation of endothelial adhesion molecules and leukocyte adhesion by treatment with superoxide dismutase is beneficial in chronic immune experimental colitis. Inflamm Bowel Dis. 2005;11(10):872–882. doi: 10.1097/01.MIB.0000183420.25186.7a. [PubMed] [CrossRef] [Google Scholar]
72. Song HY, Ju SM, Goh AR, Kwon DJ, Choi SY, Park J. Suppression of TNF-alpha-induced MMP-9 expression by a cell-permeable superoxide dismutase in keratinocytes. BMB Rep. 2011;44(7):462–467. doi: 10.5483/BMBRep.2011.44.7.462. [PubMed] [CrossRef] [Google Scholar]

73. Stamler JS, Loh E, Roddy MA, Currie KE, Creager MA. Nitric oxide regulates basal systemic and pulmonary vascular resistance in healthy humans. Circulation. 1994;89(5):2035–2040. doi: 10.1161/01.CIR.89.5.2035. [PubMed] [CrossRef] [Google Scholar]

74. Su CF, Liu DD, Kao SJ, Chen HI. Nicotinamide abrogates acute lung injury caused by ischaemia/reperfusion. Eur Respir J. 2007;30(2):199–204. doi: 10.1183/09031936.00025107. [PubMed] [CrossRef] [Google Scholar]

75. Tak PP, Firestein GS. NF-kappaB: a key role in inflammatory diseases. J Clin Invest. 2001;107(1):7–11. doi: 10.1172/JCI11830. [PMC free article] [PubMed] [CrossRef] [Google Scholar]

76. Terragni PP, Rosboch G, Tealdi A, Corno E, Menaldo E, Davini O, Gandini G, Herrmann P, Mascia L, Quintel M, Slutsky AS, Gattinoni L, Ranieri VM. Tidal hyperinflation during low tidal volume ventilation in acute respiratory distress syndrome. Am J Respir Crit Care Med. 2007;175(2):160–166. doi: 10.1164/rccm.200607-915OC. [PubMed] [CrossRef] [Google Scholar]

77. Troncy E, Collet JP, Shapiro S, Guimond JG, Blair L, Ducruet T, Francoeur M, Charbonneau M, Blaise G. Inhaled nitric oxide in acute respiratory distress syndrome: a pilot randomized controlled study. Am J Respir Crit Care Med. 1998;157(5 Pt 1):1483–1488. doi: 10.1164/ajrccm.157.5.9707090. [PubMed] [CrossRef] [Google Scholar]

78. Vaneker M, Joosten LA, Heunks LM, Snijdelaar DG, Halbertsma FJ, van Egmond J, Netea MG, van der Hoeven JG, Scheffer GJ. Low-tidal-volume mechanical ventilation induces a toll-like receptor 4-dependent inflammatory response in healthy mice. Anesthesiology. 2008;109(3):465–472. doi: 10.1097/ALN.0b013e318182aef1. [PubMed] [CrossRef] [Google Scholar]

79. Veldhuizen RA, Tremblay LN, Govindarajan A, van Rozendaal BA, Haagsman HP, Slutsky AS. Pulmonary surfactant is altered during mechanical ventilation of isolated rat lung. Crit Care Med.2000;28(7):2545–2551. doi: 10.1097/00003246-200007000-00059. [PubMed] [CrossRef] [Google Scholar]

80. Veldhuizen RA, Welk B, Harbottle R, Hearn S, Nag K, Petersen N, Possmayer F. Mechanical ventilation of isolated rat lungs changes the structure and biophysical properties of surfactant. J Appl Physiol. 2002;92(3):1169–1175. doi: 10.1152/japplphysiol.00697.2001. [PubMed] [CrossRef][Google Scholar]

81. Wagner EM. TNF-alpha induced bronchial vasoconstriction. Am J Physiol Heart Circ Physiol.2000;279(3):H946–H951. [PubMed] [Google Scholar]

82. Wu F, Tyml K, Wilson JX. iNOS expression requires NADPH oxidase-dependent redox signaling in microvascular endothelial cells. J Cell Physiol. 2008;217(1):207–214. doi:

10.1002/jcp.21495.[PMC free article] [PubMed] [CrossRef] [Google Scholar]

83. Xu J, Fan G, Chen S, Wu Y, Xu XM, Hsu CY. Methylprednisolone inhibition of TNF-alpha expression and NF-kB activation after spinal cord injury in rats. Brain Res Mol Brain Res. 1998;59(2):135–142. doi: 10.1016/S0169-328X(98)00142-9. [PubMed] [CrossRef] [Google Scholar]

84. Yasui K, Baba A. Therapeutic potential of superoxide dismutase (SOD) for resolution of inflammation.Inflamm Res. 2006;55(9):359–363. doi: 10.1007/s00011-006-5195-y. [PubMed][CrossRef][Google Scholar]

85. Yasui K, Kobayashi N, Yamazaki T, Agematsu K, Matsuzaki S, Ito S, Nakata S, Baba A, Koike K. Superoxide dismutase (SOD) as a potential inhibitory mediator of inflammation via neutrophil apoptosis.Free Radic Res. 2005;39(7):755–762. doi: 10.1080/10715760500104066. [PubMed][CrossRef][Google Scholar]

86. Yates DH. Role of exhaled nitric oxide in asthma. Immunol Cell Biol. 2001;79(2):178–190. doi: 10.1046/j.1440-1711.2001.00990.x. [PubMed] [CrossRef] [Google Scholar]

87. Yen CC, Lai YW, Chen HL, Lai CW, Lin CY, Chen W, Kuan YP, Hsu WH, Chen CM. Aerosolized human extracellular superoxide dismutase prevents hyperoxia-induced lung injury. PLoS One.2011;6(10):e26870. doi:

10.1371/journal.pone.0026870. [PMC free article] [PubMed] [CrossRef][Google Scholar]
88. Yokozawa T, Fujitsuka N, Oura H. Contribution of hydroxyl radical to the production of methylguanidine from
creatinine. Nephron. 1991;59(4):662–663. doi: 10.1159/000186664. [PubMed] [CrossRef] [Google Scholar]
89. Yoshida M, Korfhagen TR, Whitsett JA. Surfactant protein D regulates NF-kappa B and matrix metalloproteinase production in alveolar macrophages via oxidant-sensitive pathways. J Immunol.2001;166(12):7514–7519. doi: 10.4049/jimmunol.166.12.7514. [PubMed] [CrossRef] [Google Scholar]
Formats:
Article
|
PubReader
|
ePub (beta)
|
PDF (1.3M)
|
Citation
Share
 Facebook
 Twitter
 Google+
Save items

https://www.ncbi.nlm.nih.gov/pmc/articles/PMC5530466/
Add to FavoritesView more options
Similar articles in PubMed
https://www.ncbi.nlm.nih.gov/pmc/articles/PMC5530466/
High-mobility group box 1 protein is involved in the protective effect of Saquinavir on ventilation-induced lung injury in mice.[Acta Biochim Biophys Sin (Shan...]
Anti-inflammatory effects of Reduning Injection on lipopolysaccharide-induced acute lung injury of rats.[Chin J Integr Med. 2014]
Febuxostat protects rats against lipopolysaccharide-induced lung inflammation in a dose-dependent manner.[Naunyn Schmiedebergs Arch Phar...]
Extracellular superoxide dismutase in biology and medicine.[Free Radic Biol Med. 2003]
Nitric oxide and lung surfactant.[Semin Perinatol. 1996]
See reviews...See all...
Links
https://www.ncbi.nlm.nih.gov/pmc/articles/PMC5530466/
MedGen
PubMed
Taxonomy
Recent Activity
https://www.ncbi.nlm.nih.gov/pmc/articles/PMC5530466/
ClearTurn Off

Intravenous superoxide dismutase as a protective agent to prevent impairment of ...
Intravenous superoxide dismutase as a protective agent to prevent impairment of lung function induced by high tidal volume ventilation
Nature Public Health Emergency Collection. 2017; 17()
Overproduction of reactive oxygen species - obligatory or not for induction of a...
Overproduction of reactive oxygen species - obligatory or not for induction of apoptosis by anticancer drugs
Chinese Journal of Cancer Research. 2016 Aug; 28(4)383
Effects of electromagnetic fields exposure on the antioxidant defense system
Effects of electromagnetic fields exposure on the antioxidant defense system
Journal of Microscopy and Ultrastructure. Oct-Dec 2017; 5(4)167
See more...
Hospital mortality, length of stay, and preventable complications among critically ill patients before and after tele-ICU reengineering of critical care processes.[JAMA. 2011]
Ventilator-associated lung injury in patients without acute lung injury at the onset of mechanical ventilation.[Crit Care Med. 2004]
High tidal volumes in mechanically ventilated patients increase organ dysfunction after cardiac surgery.[Anesthesiology. 2012]

Low-volume ventilation causes peripheral airway injury and increased airway resistance in normal rabbits.[J Appl Physiol (1985). 2002]
Alveolar macrophages contribute to alveolar barrier dysfunction in ventilator-induced lung injury.[Am J Physiol Lung Cell Mol Physiol. 2006]
Activation of human macrophages by mechanical ventilation in vitro.[Am J Physiol. 1998]
Cyclic stretch of airway epithelium inhibits prostanoid synthesis.[Am J Physiol. 1997]
Nitric oxide inhibition of basal and neurogenic mucus secretion in ferret trachea in vitro.[Br J Pharmacol. 1996]
Pulmonary surfactant proteins A and D are potent endogenous inhibitors of lipid peroxidation and oxidative cellular injury.[J Biol Chem. 2000]
Activation of NFkB and coagulation in lung injury by hyperoxia and excessive mechanical ventilation: one more reason "low and slow" is the way to go?[Transl Res. 2009]
Therapeutic effect of Mahaenggamseok-tang on neutrophilic lung inflammation is associated with NF-κB suppression and Nrf2 activation.[J Ethnopharmacol. 2016]
Review Low-tidal-volume ventilation in the acute respiratory distress syndrome.[N Engl J Med. 2007]
See more ...
Review Extracellular superoxide dismutase: a regulator of nitric oxide bioavailability.[Lab Invest. 1996]

Cu/Zn superoxide dismutase plays important role in immune response.[J Immunol. 2003]
Peroxynitrite-mediated tyrosine nitration catalyzed by superoxide dismutase.[Arch Biochem Biophys. 1992]
Extracellular superoxide dismutase is a major determinant of nitric oxide bioavailability: in vivo and ex vivo evidence from ecSOD-deficient mice.[Circ Res. 2003]
Superoxide dismutase (SOD) as a potential inhibitory mediator of inflammation via neutrophil apoptosis.[Free Radic Res. 2005]
Review Therapeutic potential of superoxide dismutase (SOD) for resolution of inflammation.[Inflamm Res. 2006]
Attenuation of hyperoxic lung injury in rabbits with superoxide dismutase: effects on inflammatory mediators.[Acta Anaesthesiol Scand. 1995]
Mechanical ventilation of isolated rat lungs changes the structure and biophysical properties of surfactant.[J Appl Physiol (1985). 2002]
Ventilation with lower tidal volumes as compared with traditional tidal volumes for acute lung injury and the acute respiratory distress syndrome.[N Engl J Med. 2000]
Interactions of lung stretch, hyperoxia, and MIP-2 production in ventilator-induced lung injury.[J Appl Physiol (1985). 2002]
Nicotinamide abrogates acute lung injury caused by ischaemia/reperfusion.[Eur Respir J. 2007]

The effects of Eucheuma cottonii on alveolar macrophages and malondialdehyde levels in bronchoalveolar lavage fluid in chronically particulate matter 10 coal dust-exposed rats.[Iran J Basic Med Sci. 2014]
Low-tidal-volume mechanical ventilation induces a toll-like receptor 4-dependent inflammatory response in healthy mice.[Anesthesiology. 2008]
Review Malondialdehyde and thiobarbituric acid-reactivity as diagnostic indices of lipid peroxidation and peroxidative tissue injury.[Free Radic Biol Med. 1990]
Contribution of hydroxyl radical to the production of methylguanidine from creatinine.[Nephron. 1991]
Review Role of exhaled nitric oxide in asthma.[Immunol Cell Biol. 2001]
Oxidative stress and lung function.[Am J Epidemiol. 1997]
Ethyl caffeate suppresses NF-kappaB activation and its downstream inflammatory mediators, iNOS, COX-2, and PGE2 in vitro or in mouse skin.[Br J Pharmacol. 2005]
Overlapping and independent contributions of MMP2 and MMP9 to lung allergic inflammatory cell egression through decreased CC chemokines.[FASEB J. 2004]
Surfactant proteins A and D protect mice against pulmonary hypersensitivity induced by Aspergillus fumigatus antigens and allergens.[J Clin Invest. 2001]

Surfactant protein-d inhibits lung inflammation caused by ventilation in premature newborn lambs.[Am J Respir Crit Care Med. 2010]
Methylprednisolone inhibition of TNF-alpha expression and NF-kB activation after spinal cord injury in rats.[Brain Res Mol Brain Res. 1998]
Review NF-kappaB: a key role in inflammatory diseases.[J Clin Invest. 2001]
Cu/Zn superoxide dismutase plays important role in immune response.[J Immunol. 2003]
Review Therapeutic potential of superoxide dismutase (SOD) for resolution of inflammation.[Inflamm Res. 2006]
Pulmonary surfactant is altered during mechanical ventilation of isolated rat lung.[Crit Care Med. 2000]
Orgotein: a new drug for the treatment of radiation cystitis.[Curr Ther Res Clin Exp. 1975]
Review The endothelial glycocalyx: composition, functions, and visualization.[Pflugers Arch. 2007]
Review Extracellular superoxide dismutase: a regulator of nitric oxide bioavailability.[Lab Invest. 1996]
Attenuation of hyperoxic lung injury in rabbits with superoxide dismutase: effects on inflammatory mediators.[Acta Anaesthesiol Scand. 1995]
Aerosolized human extracellular superoxide dismutase prevents hyperoxia-induced lung injury.[PLoS One. 2011]
Cu/Zn-superoxide dismutase and glutathione peroxidase during aging.[Biochem Mol Biol Int. 1995]

Elevation in the ratio of Cu/Zn-superoxide dismutase to glutathione peroxidase activity induces features of cellular senescence and this effect is mediated by hydrogen peroxide.[Hum Mol Genet. 1996]
Review The role of iron in the initiation of lipid peroxidation.[Chem Phys Lipids. 1987]
Review Superoxide dismutases: role in redox signaling, vascular function, and diseases.[Antioxid Redox Signal. 2011]
Alveolar macrophages contribute to alveolar barrier dysfunction in ventilator-induced lung injury.[Am J Physiol Lung Cell Mol Physiol. 2006]
Review Vascular cell adhesion molecule-1 expression and signaling during disease: regulation by reactive oxygen species and antioxidants.[Antioxid Redox Signal. 2011]
Review Mediators of chronic obstructive pulmonary disease.[Pharmacol Rev. 2004]
See more ...
Bronchoalveolar matrix metalloproteinase 9 relates to restrictive lung function impairment in systemic sclerosis.[Respir Med. 2007]
Oxidative stress and increased type-IV collagenase levels in bronchoalveolar lavage fluid from newborn babies.[Pediatr Res. 2001]
Inhibition of matrix metalloproteinase-9 prevents neutrophilic inflammation in ventilator-induced lung injury.[Am J Physiol Lung Cell Mol Physiol. 2006]
See more ...

Human TNF-alpha in transgenic mice induces differential changes in redox status and glutathione-regulating enzymes.[FASEB J. 2002]
Tumor necrosis factor-alpha overexpression in lung disease: a single cause behind a complex phenotype.[Am J Respir Crit Care Med. 2005]
Review Role of TNFalpha in pulmonary pathophysiology.[Respir Res. 2006]
The effects of tumour necrosis factor alpha on mediator release from human lung.[Pulm Pharmacol. 1995]
TNF-alpha induced bronchial vasoconstriction.[Am J Physiol Heart Circ Physiol. 2000]
See more ...
Ventilator-induced lung injury (VILI) promotes ischemia/reperfusion lung injury (I/R) and NF-kappaB antibody attenuates both injuries.[Resuscitation. 2008]
Cyclic stretch-induced oxidative stress increases pulmonary alveolar epithelial permeability.[Am J Respir Cell Mol Biol. 2013]
Ventilation-induced chemokine and cytokine release is associated with activation of nuclear factor-kappaB and is blocked by steroids.[Am J Respir Crit Care Med. 2001]
Suppressing NF-κB and NKRF Pathways by Induced Pluripotent Stem Cell Therapy in Mice with Ventilator-Induced Lung Injury.[PLoS One. 2013]
NF-κB activation in myeloid cells mediates ventilator-induced lung injury.[Respir Res. 2013]

Toll-like receptor 4-myeloid differentiation factor 88 signaling contributes to ventilator-induced lung injury in mice.[Anesthesiology. 2010]
Impairment of autophagy decreases ventilator-induced lung injury by blockade of the NF-κB pathway.[Am J Physiol Lung Cell Mol Physiol. 2013]
See more ...
Nitric oxide regulates basal systemic and pulmonary vascular resistance in healthy humans.[Circulation. 1994]
Peroxisome proliferator-activated receptor expression is reduced in skeletal muscle in COPD.[Eur Respir J. 2007]
Review Role of nitric oxide in the pathogenesis of chronic pulmonary hypertension.[Physiol Rev. 2000]
Relative contributions of endothelial, inducible, and neuronal NOS to tone in the murine pulmonary circulation.[Am J Physiol. 1999]
Effect of adenovirus-mediated gene transfer of nitric oxide synthase on vascular reactivity of rat isolated pulmonary arteries.[Pflugers Arch. 2006]
See more ...
Alveolar macrophages contribute to alveolar barrier dysfunction in ventilator-induced lung injury.[Am J Physiol Lung Cell Mol Physiol. 2006]
Peroxynitrite-mediated tyrosine nitration catalyzed by superoxide dismutase.[Arch Biochem Biophys. 1992]
Ventilator-induced injury augments interleukin-1beta production and neutrophil sequestration in lipopolysaccharide-treated lungs.[Shock. 2007]

Role of free radicals in vascular dysfunction induced by high tidal volume ventilation.[Intensive Care Med. 2009]
Extracellular superoxide dismutase is a major determinant of nitric oxide bioavailability: in vivo and ex vivo evidence from ecSOD-deficient mice.[Circ Res. 2003]
Vascular superoxide dismutase deficiency impairs endothelial vasodilator function through direct inactivation of nitric oxide and increased lipid peroxidation.[Arterioscler Thromb Vasc Biol. 1997]
iNOS expression requires NADPH oxidase-dependent redox signaling in microvascular endothelial cells.[J Cell Physiol. 2008]
Binding and uptake of surfactant protein D by freshly isolated rat alveolar type II cells.[Am J Physiol Lung Cell Mol Physiol. 2000]
Alterations to surfactant precede physiological deterioration during high tidal volume ventilation.[Am J Physiol Lung Cell Mol Physiol. 2008]
Mechanical ventilation of isolated rat lungs changes the structure and biophysical properties of surfactant.[J Appl Physiol (1985). 2002]
See more ...
Pulmonary surfactant proteins A and D enhance neutrophil uptake of bacteria.[Am J Physiol. 1998]
Mechanical ventilation of isolated rat lungs changes the structure and biophysical properties of surfactant.[J Appl Physiol (1985). 2002]

Pulmonary surfactant proteins A and D are potent endogenous inhibitors of lipid peroxidation and oxidative cellular injury.[J Biol Chem. 2000]
Review Surfactant protein A (SP-A): the alveolus and beyond.[FASEB J. 2001]
Surfactant protein D regulates NF-kappa B and matrix metalloproteinase production in alveolar macrophages via oxidant-sensitive pathways.[J Immunol. 2001]
Surfactant protein-d inhibits lung inflammation caused by ventilation in premature newborn lambs.[Am J Respir Crit Care Med. 2010]

TRIBULATION HAS BEGUN

www.ingramcontent.com/pod-product-compliance
Lightning Source LLC
Chambersburg PA
CBHW070937180426
43192CB00039B/2316